Streetfighter Marketing

For our families:

Jeff: for Jodi, Amanda, and Mitchell

Marc: for Edye and Austin

Contents

Foreword

That person with the amazed expression on his face is *me*, amazed once again that Jeff and Marc Slutsky have, for the umpteenth time, come up with new ideas for the owners of businesses, offering them a clear, understandable, lethal plan for out-marketing their competitiors without outspending them.

The brothers Slutsky rise high above the usual marketing pap, leaving theory and tradition in the wake as they alert the business communities to realities that will truly *empower their marketing*, which is the nineties way to say generate obscenely high profits.

Right in your hands, you hold the key to *narrowcasting* instead of broadcasting, *micromarketing* instead of mass marketing, marketing from *the streets* instead of marketing from an ivory tower.

Marketing guerrillas understand the importance of community networking. Jeff and Marc put a new spin on community networking, calling it "Streetfighter Marketing" and warning you that although it is still relatively undiscovered, it is awaiting discovery by the 3 million businesses that have been launched in the U. S. since the start of 1993. This book gives you a head start on understanding it, learning how to put it to work for your business, and taking you by the hand and leading you through the successful implementation of it.

Finally, *Streetfighter Marketing* takes you far, far from the simple and expensive realm of advertising. Any dodo with money can advertise. This book shows you how to combine it with community involvement, networking, merchant certificates, special events, and many of the other weapons known to streetfighter marketing guerillas.

There seems to be an overlap between a guerrilla and a street-fighter. That overlap comes in the areas of profitability, effectiveness, and the ability of business owners to succeed in a big way. If that's to be you, this book will serve as an invaluable guide. I wish you well.

Jay Conrad Levinson
Author, *Guerilla Marketing*

Acknowledgments

We wish to thank Jeff Herman for his years of support and guidance; Beth Anderson for being a patient, persistant, and outstanding editor; and our friends and colleagues of the National Speakers Association for their help and contributions. We also want to extend a special thanks to our special friends, Bill Bishop, Carl Hammerschlag, Michael LeBoeuf, Jay Conrad Levinson, Robert L. Shook, and Ron Specht. Thanks also to the numerous companies and small businesses that generously shared their ideas and experiences with us.

1

A Global Perspective on Neighborhood Marketing

Consider the impact you could make on your business with a new weapon in your marketing arsenal. It would not replace your advertising and promotional programs but instead supplement them. This new marketing technique would give you a tremendous edge over your competition . . . a turbocharger for a marketing engine, if you will. This new approach is simple, sustainable, and gets tangible, trackable results. Besides, once developed, it costs practically nothing. Its been proven successful for both the single-unit operator and the multiple-unit operator with dozens, hundreds, or even thousands of locations nationwide. It works for retail and service providers, whether located in rural, urban, or suburban markets. This approach is used by franchises, chains, and dealership networks. And the best part is that once you've developed and implemented your program properly you've preempted your competition from using it effectively.

I call this program "Streetfighter Marketing," though it's also referred to as "neighborhood marketing" or "community networking." It may be the last untapped marketing tool that you'll find. It could mean the difference between fabulous success and mere survival for your business. It's not dependent on some new technology. Quite the contrary: elements of it have been around for hundreds of years.

Many businesses have attempted similar programs; some have marginal success, but most fail. The names of the programs vary,

1

and include Local Store Marketing (LSM), Store-Level Area Marketing (SLAM), STore Area Representation (STAR), Neighborhood Level Marketing, Network Marketing, and Relationship Marketing. None of these programs has reached its potential because each has left out important elements of the Streetfighter approach. The goal of this book is to describe a program that will ensure your business success. It provides a complete blueprint to help you win more customers and increase sales, despite a shoestring budget. But first I want to introduce the ten rules of all successful Streetfighter marketing campaigns.

The Ten Rules of Streetfighting Success

1. Focus on the neighborhood.
2. Make local marketing part of operations.
3. Make and implement decisions locally.
4. Develop from the bottom with support from the top.
5. Offer rewards and punishments.
6. Train for results.
7. Be adaptable and accountable.
8. Understand and exploit the competition.
9. Think long term and use diversity.
10. Engender cooperation among distribution channels.

1. Focus on the Neighborhood

Advertisers have exhausted every form of advertising in existence. They use television, radio, billboards, magazines, and newspapers. Thanks to cable and specialty magazines, they can reach more select groups. Advertising agencies have turned marketing into a science. But that's not enough anymore.

Now we witness an ever-increasing use of specialty media and sponsorships to gain the attention of consumers. Advertisers use direct mail, telemarketing, public relations, and publicity. Specialty advertising can put your business's name on pencils, pens, mugs, caps, and just about anything you can name to keep customers thinking about you and what you sell. Product names appear on everything, from race cars to rockets. And don't forget contests and sweepstakes, which can generate additional awareness, interest, and trial use.

You may use some very effective new distribution channels, including direct-response advertising, the Home Shopping Channel or QVC, and multilevel marketing, all of which bypass the traditional retail distribution chain. Today, for example, many of the biggest and most successful PC manufacturers are shying away from retail stores in favor of using mail order to sell their products. This marketing strategy puts computer retailers in a very uncomfortable position, while it gives a savvy manufacturer a great opportunity.

Despite all these potential marketing tools available to you, it's still tough to show a return on your advertising investment. What's the one strategy left to explore? That strategy is neighborhood marketing, a kind of "micromarketing" where you focus your effort in the area where you pull 80–90 percent of your customers. A "neighborhood" is that area with a three- to five-mile radius (that is, within a drive time of ten to twenty minutes) around a given location. The actual radius depends on the product or service you offer and conditions in the local marketplace. In addition to being effective and underutilized, neighborhood marketing is one of the least costly strategies to implement.

To illustrate, let's examine Pizza Hut, a major franchise. In the United States Pizza Hut has about 9,500 locations. Pizza Hut invests a lot of money on *national* TV advertising, Yellow Pages ads, newspaper inserts, coupon mailings, radio ads, sweepstakes and contests, consumer research, and a myriad of other promotional tools on a national, regional, and citywide level. But the success of the Pizza Hut organization is based on those 9,500 individual locations that serve 9,500 specific neighborhoods. Those specific neighborhoods are the last frontier in advertising.

Within two to three miles of a given Pizza Hut there are a host of opportunities for networking. There are hundreds of other businesses, schools, community centers, neighborhood associations, nonprofit groups, churches, and so on. If the manager or owner of a specific Pizza Hut is a trained "Streetfighter," he or she knows how to utilize the pieces of this network to attract more paying customers, increase sales, and fatten profits.

Many marketers in small towns that are dominated by nearby big-city media have used neighborhood marketing effectively for years. They had no alternative because the area media are prohibitively expensive. By contrast, few big-city marketers have realized that neighborhood marketing could also be effective for them. Whether a company has one outlet or fifty in an area, neighborhood marketing will draw customers.

A few years ago Burger King tried to go head to head with McDonalds. Burger King quickly found out that such a strategy was futile because McDonalds has twice as many locations and a significantly larger national advertising budget. Burger King couldn't beat McDonalds at its own game. But Burger King could have attempted to take on McDonalds one-on-one at the neighborhood level. In a given neighborhood you might find a McDonald's, a Burger King, a Wendy's, and maybe a local or regional fast-food competitor. The Big Three burger makers have their national advertising programs, as well as a host of other marketing programs. They've all dabbled in neighborhood marketing, but the one that learns how to utilize a fully integrated neighborhood-level marketing program will gain a big advantage in that area. Success at the neighborhood level won't negate all the dollars spent on national and regional advertising by the competitors. However, it will give one burger maker an edge in luring more customers from the other two giants.

BUT WHAT ABOUT ME?

You may be thinking that the Streetfighter Marketing strategy may be fine for a pizza or hamburger chain, but that it would have no relevance for your business. You're wrong. You'll find that no matter what product or service you offer, neighborhood marketing will work for you.

But how does Streetfighting work for major retailers, for example, a department store? First, you redefine "neighborhood" to stretch beyond the three- to five-mile radius suited to a fast-food outlet, since a department store or mass merchandiser like Wal-Mart or K-Mart will pull customers from much farther away. Second, you treat each department in a large store as if it were its own store. For example, the manager of the sporting goods department in a J.C. Penny could set up many different promotions within a twenty mile radius from his or her store to specifically promote sporting goods. Not only can each department head initiate his or her own neighborhood-level marketing program, but sometimes departments can work together both internally and externally to attract more customers.

CHICK-FIL-A AND SEARS

Chic-fil-A is a very successful fast-food food chain that specializes in chicken. Most of its outlets are located in malls. One outlet had as a regular customer the credit manager for the Sears located in the same mall. The credit manager was looking for a way to attract more credit-card applicants. The Sears credit manager ask the Chic-fil-A manager for some help because the latter was always doing creative promotions. They came up with a program that attracted over ten thousand credit-card applicants and Chic-fil-A customers. You'll learn the details of this promotion in a Chapter 2, but the point is that departments within department stores can market like their independent counterparts. Unfortunately, most big retailers keep too tight a rein on the department managers and don't allow them these opportunities. But it is possible. Neighborhood marketing works for the major players too.

WORKING THE SERVICE SIDE

How about the small operators who have a very narrow customer base? The service sector is much less reliant on geographical location since service businesses often take their service directly to the customer. For a lawn service, a stockbroker, an insurance company, a home-security company, and a host of other services, neighborhood marketing doesn't apply, unless you redefine "neighborhood" to mean a *narrow demographical area* instead of a *small geographical area*. If you're marketing life insurance you can sell it to anyone in your territory, which may have a twenty-mile radius. As the owner of a business, you know the type of people you want to reach. You select a certain segment of the market that is likely to buy the products you offer. For example, let's say you've built a niche working with people who are older, well-to-do, and looking for ways to transfer their wealth to their heirs by minimizing steep inheritance taxes. You've just described a "demographic neighborhood."

What do these people have in common? Where do they shop, vacation, buy cars, eat, live, and so on? You know that your best prospects most likely live in certain areas, belong to the same clubs, shop at the same stores, and so on. Once you've developed relationships with those other businesses and organizations that reach your target customer base you can develop promotions that use the same strategies as geographical neighborhood programs.

Regardless of your product, service, or position in the distribution chain, you'll find that a "Streetfighter Neighborhood Marketing" program gives you tremendous advantages over your competition, if you develop, implement, roll out, and maintain the program effectively. In any organization, whether Dairy Queen or Deck the Walls, Jiffy Lube or Gymboree, ReMax Realtors or H & R Block, there are perhaps a handful of managers or franchisees who actually take advantage of these opportunities. Now imagine what would happen in a company where most of its outlets were taking advantage of neighborhood marketing opportunities. Each manager or owner would network in the community and maneuver to become the dominant player in *their* business, in *that* specific neighborhood. The potential is astounding.

2. Make Marketing Part of Operations

One of the biggest mistakes executives make when they try to institute a neighborhood marketing program is that they think it's a *marketing* program that should be handled by the company's marketing people. This mistake is understandable, but nonetheless harmful. The only way a neighborhood-level marketing program will work is if it is executed from the operations side, not the marketing side. This is perhaps one of the biggest stumbling blocks to creating a successful neighborhood marketing program because marketing people and operations people always seem to be at odds with each other.

Typically, the operations people think of the marketing people as crazy troublemakers who are always looking for ways to make the operations job more difficult. The marketers, on the other hand, believe that the operations people are sabotaging their neighborhood marketing program. Marketers would say that operations people are too concerned with making sure the product quality and inventory is right, the personnel are trained, and the location is properly run, and not concerned enough about winning customers.

Despite this problem, the marketing function must not be shunted to the side. The only way to really get results from neighborhood marketing is to integrate it with operations. In a discount haircut organization, for example, the store manager would not only be responsible for hiring and firing the stylists, making sure they have enough shampoo and conditioner, seeing that the floors get swept and the bathroom gets cleaned, and so on, he or she would be responsible for weekly promotions to ensure that the shop has a steady flow of new customers. Promotion becomes part of the operation just as any new product or service becomes part of the operation. It's a line-item on the operations' checklist. The area supervisor and the district manager make sure the promotion is done and done right. The success or failure of these promotions is reflected in the supervisor's evaluation of that shop's manager and it's another element that's considered during the recruitment process.

The marketing staff's role is to make sure that the actual promotions make sense. They coordinate all the support materials, collateral advertising, and training materials needed to make the promotion work. They become a conduit for all the information from the field, so they can see what works and what doesn't. They are advisers to the operations people who have the responsibility for final implementation of a program.

In short, the operations people become experts in neighborhood marketing implementation. They become as adept with these techniques as they would be with any other vital aspect of the job of running a specific location. This expertise should start as high up the corporate ladder as possible, preferably with the vice-president for operations. All other levels of operations management must know how to implement and supervise a neighborhood marketing strategy.

3. Make and Implement Decisions Locally

To be successful, the techniques must be set up on the *local* level by the *local* management. Many organizations fight this aspect of a neighborhood marketing because they want centralized control, but centralized control smothers the initiative that makes neighborhood marketing work, and eventually, causes the program to fail.

These same organizations often want to achieve the benefits of neighborhood marketing by creating "The Manual." This neighborhood marketing handbook ties up valuable staff or ad agency resources, costs a small fortune, and produces a huge three-ring binder with every idea an operator will ever need to be successful. Many of the ideas sound good, but they haven't been field-tested. But even if the ideas are idiot-proof, what good are they? The Manual usually sits on the manager's shelf and gathers dust because he or she hasn't been properly trained and motivated to execute the programs it contains.

I remember reviewing one such manual for an automotive service franchise. One technique suggested in this manual required the manager to send a business letter to a prospective promotional partner. Obviously the people who suggested this idea never spent a minute at one of their stores because the guys in the shops had no way to write business letters. No typewriters. No word processors. Most of the time their hands are covered in grease. Not one manager followed the manual's suggestion, and the marketing geniuses at headquarters never could figure out why.

Unfortunately, even if only three or four of the manual's suggestions are useless, they will destroy the credibility of the entire program. On the other hand, if you develop the program with input from the implementor, you have a greater chance of success.

Some companies try to centralize or delegate the implementation phase. They'll hire a person and give him or her sole responsibility to create local promotions for many different stores in one area. But if the individual store managers or owners don't learn how to do their own promotions for their own stores, the program will die on the vine. To really take advantage of the vast opportunities in a neighborhood, you have to live and work there. You have to know the community and its business leaders. You have to identify the great opportunities and eliminate the timewasters. And only the person running the show, or an assistant to that person, can do that effectively. It can't be jobbed out or delegated up.

As you can imagine, there's strong resistance by executives to this concept. Many organizations want their managers to focus on operations only. They don't want them dabbling in marketing. On the other hand, organizations that discover how to meld the two effectively will have the advantage of having supplemental advertising and promotions in each of the communities where they have a store. Your organization may be one of the few that will master Streetfighter Marketing.

4. Develop from the Bottom Up, and Support from the Top Down

A neighborhood marketing program is the *last* thing you introduce at a local business. First, you have to provide a good service or a quality product. Without a first-rate service or product to offer the customer, creative neighborhood marketing will bring in more customers to see just how bad your product or service is, thereby driving you out of business all the faster. No matter what marketing you do, there's nothing that will make up for a bad product, an inferior service, and low customer satisfaction.

When a potato chip company broke into the Indianapolis market but generated just a fraction of its anticipated sales, the company hired Lee Bleifeld's marketing firm to develop an advertising campaign to get more people to buy their chips. Bleifeld started with a little reconnaissance to make sure he understood the problem before suggesting a solution.

After spending just a few days in the Indianapolis grocery stores where the chips were sold, Bleifeld's group discovered something very interesting. The distributor handling the chips made deliveries to the stores every Friday, and by Saturday the chips were sold out. The new chipmaker's biggest competitor made deliveries on Friday and then again on Saturday. They not only restocked their own shelves, but also stocked the now-empty shelfs of Bleifeld's client too.

Bleifeld's recommendation was simple: have the distributor restock the shelves again on Saturday so there would be enough chips to last the weekend. By examining the problem from the store level, as opposed to just blindly following his client's wishes, Bleifeld determined that advertising wouldn't have solved the problem. If anything, it probably would have made matters worse and wasted a lot of advertising money.

Assuming that the operation is at a level that ensures customer satisfaction, the challenge is to develop that local-level program from the *bottom* up, not the top down.

Think of the process of developing and rolling out a neighborhood marketing program as similar to the creation and introduction of a new product, service, or procedure. You start with your best research, your best guesses, and your gut instincts. But before you present this product or describe the new service at the annual meeting or at a series of regional meetings, you test it. You try it out in a couple of "test" markets for six months or a year. During that time you work out all the bugs. Then you bring it back in-house and perfect it.

Successful projects depend on selecting a couple of special markets where many of the participating managers are really sharp. These are not test markets, but rather "developmental" markets because they help to build the program. This first phase is the most difficult because it requires the participants to take generic ideas and customize them specifically for their company. Those responsible for training the developmental participants contact them regularly to find out exactly what is working and what isn't working. Sometimes it takes several months to find the exact techniques or combination of techniques to move the needle.

By the end of this development phase a company has the experience to structure each promotion in such a way as to get the most with the least. The company has results, examples, anecdotes, and company heroes to single out for praise, as well as successful prototypes from which to begin the roll-out process.

While a successful neighborhood marketing program must be developed from the bottom up, it must also be fully supported from the top down. The CEO, the company president, and all the vice-presidents have to be behind the program if it is to work. Upper management's enthusiasm for the program or the lack of such enthusiasm filters down and promotes or retards program success.

I had one very frustrating experience with a client whose development phase took place in two different markets. One was a major city where the client's company was well established and sales were already going well. The other was in a state where the client had only a few, widely spaced, newer stores; had yet to secure much public awareness; and had too little penetration in any one city to effectively use mass media.

All things being equal, the established market should have shown results much faster than the less-penetrated market. The opposite was true. Unfortunately, the area vice-president for the established market simply refused to make adjustments to the program. He didn't see a need for them: all his stores were making money, so why should he and his store managers bother?

On the other hand, the other market had far less market penetration and customer awareness. They also had a major competitor in the market who had already achieved very strong penetration. The store managers in this area and their vice-president were hungry. They followed the rules that make for a successful Streetfighter Marketing program. They knew they had a tough road to follow before they could catch up with other company stores in established markets.

After a few months I realized that the stores in the established market was not going to support the program. The CEO of the entire organization was behind the program but didn't want to force it on any of his regional vice-presidents. So I dropped the established market from the development phase and concentrated all my efforts on the other market. Meanwhile, the established market was starting to see erosion in sales because of increased competition and an anemic local economy. Had this regional vice-president understood the value of the Streetfighter program even for an established market, he not only could have increased sales and profits, but also could have made it difficult for a new competitor to gain a foothold in the community.

5. Rewards and Punishments

In all phases of neighborhood marketing program there has to be a positive reward when participants do things right and a punishment when they don't do what they're supposed to. In the example I just mentioned, where the regional vice-president opted not to support the program, there was no reward or punishment system in place to give him an incentive to even consider throwing his support behind it. To him the program just represented more work, and since things were going OK why should he put himself out? He didn't consider the possibility of what would happen if he could add additional sales over the next year. Introducing a new marketing strategy requires people to make a change and to take on additional responsibilities. The various local promotions and techniques will not always run smoothly. Some will be out-in-out flops. That's perfectly normal and part of the learning curve. It's critical, therefore, that a reward and punishment system encourages continued participation even after weak results from a particular effort. It's also critical that punishment should only be used for nonparticipation. Never punish for mistakes or failed promotions. As a matter of fact, if managers aren't making mistakes, they're not doing enough!

6. Training for Results

Perhaps the biggest mistake organizations make is that they expect their managers or owners to implement all these great ideas without training. They invite them to a seminar and then give them a book to read. The managers now have the award-winning manual on the shelf, but because they lack proper training the program falls apart. It reminds me of the movie *Karate Kid*, where the "kid" first tries to learn karate from a book. You need an instructor who knows how to effectively teach the ideas to guide you. You need someone who has been there before to help you achieve a level of proficiency you never thought you could.

Training in neighborhood-marketing techniques should be as important and intensive as any other aspect of the operation if you wish a neighborhood program to be successful. Many people who will be trained in these techniques have no sales experience. They don't know who to see or what to say. The training program, therefore, includes role-playing so they get used to presenting the program to the right people.

It's also important that your program allows for every contingency: a grand opening, competitive intrusion, competitive exit, remodeling, road construction near the location, management turnover, bad press, natural disaster, and so on. It's very likely that each of your locations will experience one or more of these situations. Instead of shooting from the hip or, worse, doing nothing when these problems occur, you need to have programs in place to minimize damage and perhaps even take advantage of opportunity.

I consulted with a client who owned a chain of thirty family restaurants, several of which were located in Indianapolis. A couple of months after the grand opening of one of his stores, the street in front was completely torn up, making it inconvenient for customers to visit. For weeks the staff blamed the construction workers for their slow sales, but of course that tactic accomplished nothing. I suggested that they try to make allies of the workers who are outside just doing their job. I said, "Bring them out free coffee and invite them in for some free appetizers." By getting the workers on their side, as it were, the workers could reduce some of the customers' negative feelings. When a customer was interested in visiting the restaurant, the workers would go out of their way to make it easier for them to get past the barriers, even to the extent of stopping oncoming traffic. The goal was to lessen the effect of a negative situation. A trained Streetfighting store manager would have known what to do immediately and dealt with the situation.

7. Be Flexible and Accountable

One significant change in corporate attitudes that has affected the success of some neighborhood marketing programs is allowing the local managers to make decision on their own. There are strong guidelines in place and the managers do have training to deal with almost any situation or opportunity, so giving them freedom shouldn't be as scary as it sounds. The "Mother-May-I?" mentality is a sure way to kill a neighborhood marketing program. By the same token, the managers who take on the responsibility for decision making should be held accountable for their actions. When they implement programs, their results should be tracked. The promotions must be the type that get measurable results. To say "We got some great PR" or "We created goodwill in the community" in not enough. When a manager, owner, or dealer spends time and money on something, there needs to be tangible, trackable results.

There also has to be some tolerance for mistakes. If a manager is afraid that a promotion's failure will result in punishment from the boss, he or she will never try anything new. But if the company encourages risk taking and innovation, employees will learn from their mistakes and successes. Some companies have gone so far as to award prizes for the biggest blunder. Have fun with implementing and building a program. Learn from failures and use them as a way to encourage future success for the entire chain. The only activity that should be punished is inactivity.

8. Understanding the Competition

Your competition in a constant state of change, giving your customers many more choices where to spend their money. Sometimes you're not even aware of whom your competition really is. When I started doing a series of workshops for Marvel Entertainment, I was introduced to the retailers by their sales manager, Bruce. He told me that in years past they had spent a lot of money providing the retailers with all kinds of "trinkets" like key chains, baseball caps, pens, and so on. However, this year the company had decided to spend that money on bringing them me. What a rude awakening! My competition in this case wasn't another speaker or trainer. Imagine how I felt when I realized that I was a substitute for coffee mug or an ice scraper.

I also remember the time a competitor turned into an ally. In the course of contacting potential clients around the country to inquire about using me as their keynote speaker at their annual convention, I discovered that one of my biggest competitors was speaker/author Jay Conrad Levinson, author of the *Guerilla Marketing* series. Every time I lost an engagement to Jay I got upset. My salespeople got upset. We thought of Jay as the enemy.

Then, one day I decided to give Jay a call to satisfy my curiosity. I had remembered one of my favorite quotes from the movie *Godfather II*: "Keep your friends close but your enemies closer." I called Jay up and introduced myself and he exclaimed, "Jeff Slutsky! I love your stuff. I quote you in my seminar." Well, immediately my opinion of Jay changed. He thought it would make sense for us to network together since after he's done giving a seminar for a client he has no follow-up program. We could refer business back and forth and so on. I was quoted in his *Guerilla Selling* book, and he has written the Foreword and provided me with some great examples for this book.

The same principle applies on the local level. There are times when a store or office should network with a direct competitor to increase sales. Sometimes owners or managers look at competitors and see them as a much greater threat than they really are. And sometimes they look at another business and don't even see that they are taking more customers from that business than that business is taking from them.

For example, consider a full-service car wash. Who is the competitor? Of course, it's other car washes and people who wash their own cars. But there is also another, not-so-obvious major competitor: the nonprofit groups who hold car washes to raise money for their worthy causes. Although the owner of the car wash recognizes that the nonprofit car washes are for charity, he also knows that these groups are cutting into his profits. Instead of getting upset, a Streetfighter finds a way to become an ally to these groups. By encouraging fundraising promotions for nonprofit groups whose events are held at his car wash, he creates an "everyone wins" situation. One possibility might be to have the nonprofit group distribute special certificates in the community. The customer pays the regular full price for his or her car wash. But when he or she submits the certificate with the payment, the car-wash owner donates a certain sum to the fundraising group. The car-wash owner gets a number of customers who might not have come to his business. He also gets a "good guy" image in his marketplace. Plus, he removes a little bit of competition at the same time. This is just one very simplified example, but it gives you an indication about how to look at competition differently. This and other promotions like it are described in greater detail in later chapters.

9. *Think Long Term*

Neighborhood marketing is a dynamic program. Once developed and rolled out, it can be adapted and improved indefinitely. Unfortunately most companies insist on instant gratification from their marketing. Their experience is to launch a major media campaign and get results immediately. When they need another sales boost three months later, they launch another campaign or have a contest. Neighborhood marketing takes a more long-term view. But with some patience, the company that practices neighborhood marketing will witness long-term, sustainable results.

A variety of ideas are necessary for success. No one promotion or no one type of promotion can exploit the potential market alone. There is a synergistic effect, which, over time, and by using many different types of promotions, creates the ultimate impact in that community. Some promotions may be huge successes. Some might bomb. There will be variety of other promotions that will be marginally successful. All contribute to the total success of the program.

10. Engender Cooperation among All Channels of Distribution

Increasingly, manufacturers and wholesalers are discovering that if their retailers don't do a good job of running their business, they all sell fewer products and services. Franchisors are painfully aware that if their franchisees are not successful, their ability to sell more franchises and increase the revenues they receive from royalty payments is greatly jeopardized. Major vendors to retailers, like credit-card companies, are keenly aware that if their clients' sales slump, their sales suffer too.

For example, Marvel Entertainment is the largest comic-book publisher. Its market share, at this writing, is two to three times that of their nearest competitors, DC and Image. A significant part of Marvel's revenues comes from the sale of comic books through five thousand independent, specialty comic-book stores. The vast majority of the proprietors, while having tremendous product knowledge, lacked the basic business skills of marketing, advertising, promotion, and sales. As a result, Marvel hired us to develop a "Streetfighting" program for comic-book stores. The training the store owners and managers received helped many of them sell more comic books, which of course, benefited Marvel.

It's interesting to note that Marvel didn't go it alone. The company worked very closely with the major comic-book distributors, such as Capital City, Diamond, and Hero's World, so that they too could be a hero to their clients. Marvel paid for the development, presentations, and materials, but the training sessions were conducted at events put on by these distributors. It's this cooperative relationship between all the distribution channels, (in this case, publisher, distributor, and retailer), that allowed independent retailers to benefit from the program.

The Future of Neighborhood Marketing

The remainder of this book will help you understand all of the details of putting together an effective neighborhood marketing program. You'll read about actual promotions, done by a wide variety of businesses, and also about how the development and training process works.

Imagine each one of your locations' managers conducting one low-cost promotion, each and every week, forever. In a five-hundred-location chain, for example, over twenty-five thousand local promotions will take place in the first year. That's besides any national, regional, and citywide promotions and advertising you're already doing.

Your local management will be energized through controlling their own destiny and making things happen. You'll have five hundred managers with the drive of an entrepreneur and the discipline and direction of a corporate executive. You will own the turf around each store. No matter what any competitor does, short of giving away their stores, your stores can counter head to head.

2

Building Your Neighborhood Sales with Merchant Networking

In nearly any neighborhood there are hundreds of opportunities to get either free or low-cost distribution of your promotional and advertising messages. These opportunities generally fall into ten different categories, which could be called the *Ten Avenues of Free Distribution*:

1. Retail merchants
2. Major employers
3. Educational institutions
4. Associations and organizations
5. Events and celebrations
6. Your employees
7. Your customers
8. Business-to-business merchants
9. Nonprofit groups
10. News media

Cross-promotion is a broad-based term used to describe any type of marketing in which two different organizations help promote each other. The type of cross-promotion that has application for most businesses is what Streetfighters refer to as the "merchant certificate exchange." The goal of this promotion is to get other merchants in your neighborhood to handout *your* advertising to *their* customers, for *free*.

When the movie *Batman Returns*, the sequel to the original *Bat-*

FIGURE 2–1

This exceptional cross-promotion generated more than $30,000 in
twelve months.

man movie, was released, Jayson Lynk, the manager of Big League
Sports, a comic-book store in Warren, Ohio, saw an opportunity
for a merchant-certificate type of cross-promotion. Lynk reasoned
that, while not everyone who would go to the movie would be a
comic-book buyer, nearly everybody who does buy comic books
would go to see *Batman Returns*. Because of the major competition
in his area for those comic-book customers, he wanted to do something very special.

He approached the manager of the biggest movie theater in the
area. He first suggested trading some free movie passes for gift certificates at his store that could be used for employee incentives and
customer door prizes. He then suggested that they display each
other's posters. Lastly, Lynk provided the movie-theater owner
with a batch of special cross-promotion certificate good for $1 off
the purchase of $10 or more of any Batman products in his store.
Each person who bought a ticket to *Batman Returns* received one

of these certificates; over 10,000 were distributed. (See Figure 2–1.)

Out of the 10,000 certificates distributed, 150 were redeemed. That's just a 1.5 percent return, apparently not very good until you look at it from a return-on-investment standpoint. Those 150 people had to buy at least $1,500 worth of merchandise. Even better, about 50 of those people became Lynk's regular customers. Comic-book readers often visit a comic-book store every week to keep current with their favorite titles. Lynk figures that his regular customers spend an average of $10 per visit. When you do the math, you discover that this one promotion generated over $26,000 for Lynk in the first year. But that's not all! One of those new customers was a twelve-year-old boy who showed up in a chauffeur-driven limousine. Accompanied by his personal nanny, he spent no less than $300 a week. On his birthday that year he spent over $3,000. Can you imagine how much he'll spend the year after his bar mitzvah? The bottom line on this promotion was a $30,000+ increase in sales the first year.

One year later most of those new customers were still spending their $10 per week in Lynk's store. When *Jurassic Park* opened at the same theater, Lynk organized a similar promotion. David Rarick of Stand Up Comics in Circleville, Ohio, was thinking along the same lines when he teamed up with Circle Cinema, the only movie theater in his town. After his wife, a graphic designer, worked up a draft of the certificate he wanted to distribute (see Figure 2–2),

FIGURE 2–2
Cross-promotions excel when you work with the right promotional partner at the right time.

Rarick approached the manager of the Circle Cinema. The manager enthusiastically agreed to distribute the certificate in return for Rarick's promise to put a sign near his *Jurassic Park* display reading "Now Playing at the Circle Cinema."

Jayson Lynk, David Rarick, and many other comic-book retailers as well as traditional booksellers across the nation are looking forward to the promotions opportunities that new *Spiderman, Fantastic Four*, and *X-Men* movies will present.

Since many of these movies are so well merchandised, another major cross-promotion partner could be held with a toy store. Also, it's likely that one of the major fast-food chains will pick up on some of them, so comic-book stores should look for neighborhood opportunities with them too.

A merchant promotion doesn't always have to include a piece of printed advertising that is distributed to customers, though I believe that such advertising produces better results. Nonetheless, simply using another business to give your own business more exposure provides you with an opportunity to attract new customers at little or no cost to you.

An East Coast scuba-diving center with a customer base of affluent people who could afford to spend thousands of dollars on scuba equipment and trips to the Great Barrier Reef in Australia or the Red Sea in Israel did a cross-promotion with a restaurant that attracted many new customers. Their demographic target audience was made up of yuppies, DINKS (dual income, no kids) and OINKS (one income, no kids). One local business that appeared to cater to the same type of people was an upscale seafood restaurant. Also, since it was a seafood restaurant the theme of the promotion tied in very nicely with the scuba-diving center.

The diving center put a display in the restaurant lobby featuring scuba gear and continuous videos of exotic underwater dives. A poster indicated who was responsible for the display and brochures provided interested parties with information about the center's services, including their diving courses. On busy weekends there was a captive audience in the restaurant lobby, people were glad to watch the diving videos while waiting for their tables. The display cost almost nothing. The restaurant loved it because it created something of interest in their lobby at no cost to them. Everyone won.

In this particular promotion, no special certificate was given to the restaurant's customers. The promotion might have gotten a better response if each customer got a "Discover Scuba" invitation allowing him or her a free scuba-diving lesson. That one addition to the promotion might have provided the little extra incentive to prompt more of the restaurant's customers to give scuba diving a try, and it would have allowed the diving center to track the number of customers that the restaurant promotion generated.

Basically, the whole idea behind a cross-promotion is to get someone else, someone who has contact with people whom you want as your customers, to distribute your advertising for you, for free. To be most successful, you must choose a promotional partner that already has a strong customer base consisting of that specialized audience that has reason to be interested in what you have to offer. The specialized groups comic-book buyers and people with large discretionary recreational budgets have relatively few members in terms of the total population, yet, by looking in logical places, you can attract the attention of members of these specialized groups or any others you might want to reach.

The Three C's of Cross-Promotions

The elements that make cross-promotions so successful are best represented by the *Three C's of Cross-Promotions*:

Cost
Control
Credibility

Cost

There are two different benefits to the cost element of a cross-promotion: free distribution and low-cost production.

FREE DISTRIBUTION

The most expensive element of most advertising is the cost of distributing the advertising message. Generally, the cost of creating that message is only a fraction of what it costs to put that message on TV or radio, in the paper, on a billboard, or in a mailing. With a cross-promotion, you get your advertising message distributed for free.

LOW-COST PRODUCTION

The production of a cross-promotion doesn't have to be expensive. Most applications use quick printing, with black ink on colored 20-pound paper. This is very inexpensive. To have impact with a mass mailing or an insert in the newspaper, however, you have to do something to make your message stand out. So you pay for full-color printing, scratch and sniff, lick and stick, and every other gimmick you can think of. With a cross-promotion, on the other hand, because of the unique environment in which it is distributed, you don't need to go to that expense. Of course, there are exceptions to this rule. A white-tablecloth restaurant is one kind of business that should use a classier piece. In this case, the piece might be printed on a higher quality paper, engraved, and perhaps designed to look similar to a wedding invitation. A bank branch might want to print with two colors on a textured or coated paper stock to give its piece more class. Whatever the printing quality, you want your artwork to be very professional. A professionally designed, typeset, and pasted-up piece will still look professional even if printed in black ink on basic colored paper.

Control

Control is another feature of cross-promotional activity that provides you with great results, when it is done properly. By "control" I'm referring to the ability to control the audience to whom your message is distributed.

There are five types of promotional control:

1. Geographic
2. Demographic
3. Numerical
4. Competitive
5. Synergistic

GEOGRAPHIC CONTROL

For any type of retail operation, this is the type of control you most need. It allows you to focus your efforts in the neighborhood from which you pull the vast majority of your customers. A bank branch, for example, pulls customers from close to the location. To get more customers, therefore, it makes sense to find some cross-promotion partners who serve the same people you want to reach.

While you may want to focus your distribution in your neighborhood, you probably do not want to cross-promote next door. If your business is well established, it's likely that most of the customers of the business next door who could be your customers are already your customers. It doesn't make sense to offer a discount to customers you already have who are paying your regular price. But, during a slow time of the year, or when you are introducing a new product or service, or if your volume is very low for any reason, you may have good reasons to promote next door.

You have to achieve a balance. The farther away you go from your store, the greater the chance you have to find new potential customers. But at the same time, the farther away you get from your store in your search for new customers, the more difficult it becomes to lure those customers to you, especially if your competitor is closer. So, by cross-promoting with a business that's located five miles from you, your redemption level will likely be lower than a similar effort with a business located just a couple of miles away. Yet, of those people who do redeem, the percentage of new customers should be higher.

Suppose you have a competitor located three miles west from you. All things being equal, you're more likely to get those customers coming from east of your store, while your competitor is more likely to attract those coming from west of his store. The customers you're really competing for are the ones located west of you and east of him in the overlap area. To attract some of your competitor's customers from this overlap area, you should select a promotional partner located just to the east of your competitor. That will win you many of your competitor's customers, while cutting down on discounts to your regular customers.

Geographic control also means you can expand your promotion beyond the neighborhood. If you run a multiple-unit operation,

FIGURE 2–3
Map of Neighborhood

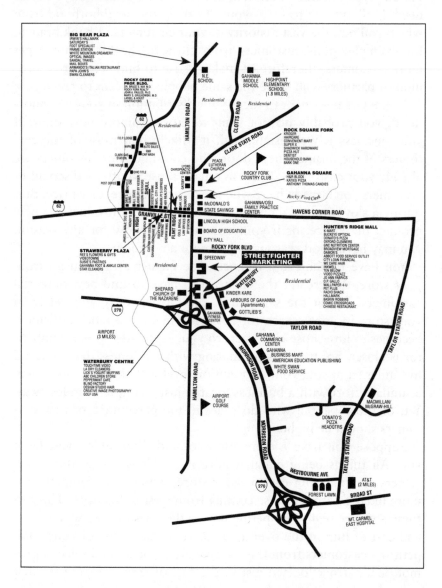

you may be able to find other multiple-unit promotional partners who could help promote many stores in your organization. It's possible to expand a promotion to a citywide, a regional, or even a national scope if it makes sense for the two promotional partners.

The neighborhood mapped in Figure 2–3 is similar to many neighborhoods. This neighborhood happens to be the one where our office and homes are located, in Gahanna, Ohio, a suburb of Columbus near the airport on the east side of town. The map shows a typical mix of chains, franchises, and independent businesses, as well as a typical assortment of schools, churches, shopping centers, government agencies, and so on.

A Streetfighter should have an intimate understanding of just about everything in his or her community. In the area just off the map to the north, there are some major new businesses including a Mejers Hyperstore and a Sears Hardware store, some new apartment complexes, and a United Diary Farmers convenience store; moreover, a large shopping center will be built in that area in a year or so. To the northeast, again just off the map, is the corporate headquarters of The Limited, a Toyota dealership, Interstate 270, which circles Columbus.

This information is important if you owned a business located in the area the map covers. For example, the Baskin Robbins located near K-Mart in the Hunter's Ridge Mall just a block north of our office attracts an entirely different group of customers than the Dairy Queen located on Highway 62 just east of Hamilton Road. You might think that the two ice cream stores would be strong competitors, but they really don't compete very much. The Dairy Queen is a free-standing building with a drive-through window, right in the heart of Gahanna, while the Baskin Robbins is located, in a shopping center, at the outskirts of town. The Dairy Queen pulls more customers from the north side of Gahanna, whereas the Baskin Robbins pulls a lot of its customers from the southern area of the community. The overlap area between the two is where the fiercest promotional battles could be fought.

If the Dairy Queen wanted to reach a greater number of potential new customers with a value offer of some kind, they would probably want to promote south of the Baskin Robbins. For example, they could approach the Gahanna Fitness Center to promote their nonfat frozen yogurt products.

Gahanna is only one of a number of communities that make up the Greater Columbus ADI.[2] In addition to Gahanna there is Reynoldsberg, Westerville, New Albany, Dublin, Hilliard, Whitehall, Bexley, Upper Arlington, Worthington, German Village, Delaware, Lancaster, Marysville, and many others.

Each of these communities is a distinct neighborhood, yet for multiple-unit operators, they are also connected. Cross-promotions and all forms of Streetfighter Marketing can be utilized at any level. Much of the time your promotional efforts will be focused on the neighborhood level. However, there are effective ways to transcend the neighborhood level, to market in in two or three neighborhoods at once, to go citywide, regionwide, or even nationwide.

Such was the case with a cross-promotion created by Minit Lube, an oil-change franchise, and Skippers, a fast-food fish chain. It started out as a single cross-promotion between a Minit Lube and a Skippers located in the same neighborhood. The success of this single promotion attracted the attention of the Skippers headquarters in Seattle, and Skippers' management got in touch with Minit Lube's management and suggested duplicating the cross-promotion in all the areas where both companies had locations. Eventually,

FIGURE 2–4

With a Two-Way promotion you don't have to have an offer or value on the piece. Skippers reinforced their TV campaign in this example.

A Special "Thank You" For Our Customers . . .

Skipper§®

LOOK FOR THE STRIPES™

minit-lube®

SAVE $2.00

This special "thank you" entitles you to a $2 savings on the regular price of a full service lubrication only at the following Minit-Lube locations:

AT ANY LOCATION

Cannot be combined with any other offer. Only one special "thank you" per person per visit.

No appointment necessary   Expires: 10/31/86

FREE FRIES OR CHOWDER WITH A NEW SKIPPER'S® SANDWICH

Skipper's has three great new sandwiches;
• Double Fish with Cheese
• Chicken Tenderloin with Cheese
• Shrimp Salad Pita

Now, when you buy any of these bountiful sandwiches Skipper's will give you a FREE order of fries or cup of chowder — your pleasure.

So, even if you only have a "minit", drive by for one of Skipper's new sandwiches. They're one more tasty reason to sandwich Skipper's into your busy schedule.

offer ends 9/21/86

Skipper§®   minit-lube®

forty Skippers and twenty-eight Minit Lubes distributed each other's certificates (see Figure 2–4), some seventy thousand pieces in all. (This is a variation of the cross-promotion called a "Two-Way" discussed below.)

This is a good illustration of why not only individual store managers, but regional and district-level managers need to be familiar with all the facets of Streetfighter Marketing. Multiple-unit operations have dozens of opportunities each year to expand successful neighborhood-level promotions to the citywide, statewide, regional, or even national levels.

Special Geography. If you have a business that attracts customers only because of special circumstances, you need to look for special promotional partners. Such was the case of the McDonalds located at the airport outside Gahanna. People who worked at or who passed through the airport often visited this McDonald's, but the restaurant needed a larger customer base. To draw customers from outside the airport McDonalds instituted a cross-promotion with the Uniglobe Travel Agency. The McDonald's coupon (see Figure 2–5) was inserted in the ticket envelopes for all Uniglobe's travel customers.

DEMOGRAPHIC CONTROL

A cross-promotion allows you to focus your effort on a very narrow target audience. To do this, you first must identify other potential cross-promotion partners in your area who reach the same people you want. Jayson Lynk knew that *Batman Returns* was likely to attract a large number of people who buy comic books. A bookstore selling several *Jurassic Park* books (the novel itself, the nonfiction story of how the movie was made, children's versions of the story, coloring books, and so on) plus other dinosaur titles would do well to cross-promote with movie theaters showing that movie. A toy store could do the same (and it might want to push some of its "Barney" items at the same time).

For businesses that have a broader appeal, a restaurant, for example, or a service station, you still can benefit from this demographic control. The example of the Diary Queen and Gahanna Fitness Center's cross-promotion of a low-fat product actually represents a combination of geographic and demographic control. If a

FIGURE 2–5
This promotion targeted customers going to the airport.

sub shop does a lot of business with adults, but little business with teenagers, and wants to increase teen business, its owner should first determine what area businesses serve that group. The owner would do well to cross-promote with a music store, an arcade, an athletic shoe store, a movie theater, a comic-book store, or a clothing store that sells to teens. These cross-promotion partners would tend to reach the teenage target audience the sub-shop owner wants to tap into.

An automotive service business like a tire store, muffler store, or brake shop would want to go after a different target audience. It would be looking for adults eighteen and older or perhaps males aged eighteen to fifty-four. With this broad target spectrum you again begin by identifying those potential partners in your neighborhood that would reach those people. Some that immediately come to mind include a full-service car wash, a convenience store, a high-volume fast-food restaurant with a drive-through window, a bank branch, an auto paint shop like Maaco, a dry cleaners, a golf shop, and a sports bar. Of course, there are dozens and dozens of others.

An adult women's clothing store like a Limited, Henry Bendels, or Petite Sophisticate can target many of their potential customers by cross-promoting with Jenny Craig Weight Loss Centers, women's shoe stores (in the mall and outside of the mall), hair salons, cosmetic counters at department stores, and auto dealers that make an attempt to appeal to women (like Performance Toyota in my neighborhood).

Take the case of Doug Owens, a personal trainer. He was specifically looking for clients who could train during the middle of the day since his early mornings, evenings, and Saturdays were totally booked. Hoping to attract housewives, he did a promotion with a hair salon. The salon only handed out a couple dozen pieces offering one half-hour training session for free (see Figure 2–6). He only had one taker, but she signed up for services that netted him about $750 per year. Based on Owens's $20 investment, this was a pretty good return. To find more clients, Owens offered to provide a free lecture for a women's charity organization. Everyone in attendance was given a coupon for "one free training session."

Vendor Distribution. Sometimes you can get your vendors to promote you, and because you are their customer your promotional piece doesn't have to include an offer. Your vendors are motivated to help you because they want to keep your business. I did this when my last book, *How to Get Clients*, was released. My main target audience was small businesses, which meant I needed demographic

FIGURE 2–6
This promotion targets a group who would be free to work out at midday.

control for my promotion; location wasn't critical since the book was available through bookstores. So I had both full-sheet 8 1/2 x 11 fliers and one-third-sheet fliers printed. Then I asked two of my key, high-volume vendors to hand out my fliers to their customers. My printer distributed my larger flier to every customer, while my travel agent inserted by one-third-sheet flier (see Figure 2–7) in each of the agency's ticket envelopes for well over a month. This book promotion was merely an announcement, directing the customers to go to their bookstore to buy my book; no special offer was included.

NUMERICAL CONTROL

In this system you control the number of pieces that go out. If you want to limit the number of pieces that get distributed during a promotion, you can do so. Let's say that you're introducing a new

FIGURE 2–7
My travel agent inserted this in each ticket envelope for a month.

product or service, or perhaps it's a particularly slow time of the year for you. In these situations you may want to run a very high-value or deep-discount offer. This offer may be so attractive that you would like to limit the number of pieces that go out to advertise it. So, you have your partner simply distribute the amount you want. If that cross-promotion partner has, say, five thousand weekly customers, but you only want two thousand pieces distributed, have that partner hand them out only over the weekend or until the pieces are all gone.

This control also gives you the option of choosing those cross-promotion partners who will distribute enough volume of your advertising pieces to make some real impact.

If a certain business has fewer than a hundred weekly customers, it might not be worth it for you to arrange an official promotion. The numbers just aren't there. Some of the most successful cross-promotions are done with partners with huge customer counts. A Wag's in Port St. Lucie, Florida got the biggest return on a promotion the manager set up with a Wal-Mart down the street. Wal-Mart distributed ten thousand pieces at the cash registers in just one week. As a result the Wag's customer count went way up and sales did too.

COMPETITIVE CONTROL

This means that your competition has no idea what you're doing. You can be sure your competitors are looking for your ads in the

FIGURE 2–8

High-volume promotional partners can make a big impact in your sales.

newspaper and listening for them on the radio, but they'll probably never notice your flyers or cross-promotion certificates. This "covert" feature allows you to gain a complete foothold in your neighborhood before your rivals can do anything about it.

SYNERGISTIC CONTROL

Synergistic control usually falls into two different categories: combination synergy or accumulation synergy.

Combination Synergy. Those cross-promotions that literally blow the doors off usually combine all the other four controls. I think the main reason the *Batman Returns*/comic-book cross-promotion was so successful was its combination of "controls." First, a large volume, ten thousand pieces, was handed out during the run of the movie; this represents numerical control. Second, that movie attracted perhaps 100 percent of a narrowly defined group, the comic-book buying public (demographic control). Third, the two businesses were located only two miles apart (geographic control). And lastly, once the promotion was set up, none of the other comic-book retailers could do the same with that theater (competitive control). Lynk had preempted the competition from doing the same thing in his area.

The more narrow your target audience, the more often synergistic control comes into play. A family restaurant can target a very wide group of customers because everybody has to eat. Wal-Mart attracts a variety of customers; it's not very targeted from a cross-promotion standpoint. So when Wal-Mart hands out ten thousand pieces for a family restaurant, that's bound to have an influence on the restaurant's sales. If that same Wal-Mart handed out pieces for a comic-book store or a dive center, the response would not be as strong because each of those businesses has a more narrow appeal. They may still gain some business from such a promotion, but they would be better off to find a more targeted cross-promotion partner.

If you have any one of these controls working for you, you're likely to pick up a few customers for your effort. That's good. But every once in a while there's an opportunity to blow the doors off, and you must be ready to seize it. It usually doesn't happen often, but when the circumstances are right, you have to be ready.

Accumulation Synergy. There's one other aspect of synergistic control, the cumulative effect of many different promotions over time, as I mentioned in Chapter 1. You may only have a "grand slam" promotion once or twice a year. Or you may find that in your situation the grand-slam opportunity just doesn't exist. But you can still benefit from the cumulative effect associated with a couple of dozen different promotions. It takes longer and involves more effort, but this strategy will have a major impact on your sales.

Credibility

Credibility, the third of the three C's, is another feature of a cross-promotion. There are two types of credibility: price credibility and testimonial credibility.

PRICE CREDIBILITY

This feature has become even more important over the years. As competition increases dramatically, consumers are barraged with all kinds of off-price marketing. Coupons, sales, discount clubs, give-aways, and special financing are some ways of attracting customers. These devices condition customers to wait for a deal before they buy.

When a business puts a coupon in the paper every week, its customers come to expect that coupon. If the coupon doesn't appear one week, the customer will wait for the coupon. Many customers will not shop until the coupon appears. There's no doubt in their minds that you paid for advertising space in the past to discount your own product or service and that you will do so again. And if you don't, many of those customers will stop visiting you.

With a cross-promotion you can give someone else the credit for the deal you are offering. When the comic-book enthusiasts received that special certificate from the movie theater, the piece said that it was "compliments of National Theatre Corp." It was perceived as a gift from the theater and the movie theater got full credit for the discount. That means that once the customers got their comic-book discounts on their first visit, they were not as likely to expect another discount on their next visit. The owner of the comic-book store protects his price credibility by transferring the responsibility to the movie theater, his cross-promotion partner.

One of the major pizza chains started a delivery service in Columbus, Ohio. To order, you simply dial one number and then the pizza is dispatched from whichever of their twenty locations is located closest to you. The system is a boon to the customer, who doesn't have to look at their full-page ad in the Yellow Pages and try to figure out which location is closest. It was during one of these calls that this chain totally destroyed its price credibility with me.

I called up and the first thing the order clerk asked for was my phone number. So I gave it to her. Then I heard some clicking sounds from a computer keyboard. She said, "Oh, Mr. Slutsky. How are you today?," as if she were a flight attendant. Then she continued: "Let's see, the last time you ordered a small, mushroom, onion, and extra cheese. You paid the drive in cash. Would you like to place that same order again today?" I was a little overwhelmed by all the information she had on me, so I asked her if she'd like to do my tax returns this year. No response.

I placed my order, and then she asked me if I had any coupons. Now I was upset. She'd just informed me that everybody else in the world was paying less money for their pizza than I was. I then responded, "Do you take other people's coupons?" She told me, proudly, that they would take anyone's coupons! I said, "Great! I have a Jiffy Lube coupon!"

She took it. The deliverer came to my door with a small mushroom, onion, and extra cheese. I handed him my coupon for $3 off an oil change and he took $3 off my bill. I will never pay full price at that pizza place again because they convinced me that their regular price means nothing. They've lost all their "price credibility."

TESTIMONIAL CREDIBILITY

When a customer receives a special value certificate as part of a purchase, there is perceived value in the piece. It says to that customer, in effect, that "you are a valued customer and I'm doing something special for you. Here's a savings or a value-added for you the next time you visit this other business."

Cross-Promoting with Vendors

Sometimes you might be able to work out a cross-promotion on a larger scale with a major company. Greg Deskin of Beach City Scuba in Dana Point, California, created a promotion with American Express Travel that took him almost a year to set up but has been giving him great results. When a customer bought a Club Med vacation from American Express Travel, they gave the customer a certificate good for free scuba lessons at Beach City Scuba. Their lessons included classroom training and confined water training. After finishing these lessons, the customer only needed open water training to receive PADI certification, and this they could do at Club Med with a few lessons. American Express Travel paid Deskin for each student he enrolled. He doubled the number of his students with this unique cross-promotion.

It took Deskin about a year to put this promotion together. He first approached Club Med with his idea, but they turned him down. He then tried a number of travel agents, who also turned him down. Then American Express Travel saw the value in his program and jumped on it right away. Unlike most cross-promotions, however, this one is an ongoing promotion.

Chapter Summary

Cross-promotions are effective when done properly because they provide you free distribution of your message, allow you to target your promotion where it does you the most good, and keep you from getting a "discount" image.

The retail merchant certificate is a type of cross-promotion that helps you reach new customers by getting other merchants in your neighborhood to hand out your promotional pieces to their customers.

These promotions are most effective when your pieces are distributed by merchants whose geographic location is within a three- to five-mile radius of your store, their customer demographics are compatible with yours, and their customer counts are significant.

3

How to Set Up Your Merchant Certificate Promotion

Before you can set up your initial merchant certificate cross-promotion you first have to know which merchants to approach with your promotion. The most effective and efficient way to do this is to start with those merchants who are already your customers. Starting with your own customers provides three advantages:

1. They already know your business, so they're more likely to agree to take part in the promotion.
2. They already visit your business, so you don't have to waste valuable time by leaving your business.
3. They're more likely to execute their part of the promotion properly.

Ways to Discover Potential Cross-Promotion Partners

Business-Card Drawing

A business-card drawing is the easiest and least expensive way to find out which of your customers could be powerful cross-promotion partners. You simply put a fishbowl on the front counter and ask your business customers to deposit their businesscards for a free-prize drawing. The free prize doesn't have to be expensive, merely nice enough to prompt people to participate in the contest. You can offer some service or product you sell. After four weeks you draw your winner and award the prize. But the real prize is yours: the names, titles, business addresses, and phone numbers of your customers. You'll want to save all these cards because you'll use them for a little bit of Streetfighter research using a technique called a "scattergram," where the addresses are plotted on a map to show you where you have your customer concentrated.

Drive-By

There are many major opportunities where the store owner or manager is not your customer . . . yet. To get an idea of what's out there, take a drive through your neighborhood. You may discover a small factory with three hundred employees tucked away off the beaten path, but not far from your location. You might try driving a different way to and from work every day for a week or two. Get to know your turf.

When doing your drive-by you'll want to have paper and pen handy to write down the names of all the opportunities in your area. The process will be easier and safer if you use a hand-held recorder; then when you get back to your store, you can write down the information.

Once you've completed your business-card drawing and/or your drive-by, you need to select a number of merchants who you feel would make a good cross-promotion partner. Out of that group separate the retail merchants from the rest. From the group of retail merchants select ten you already know by sight or by name and who are likely to visit your business in the very near future. Ten is an easy number of stores to keep track of, though you could choose any number you wish. You'll eventually use many more then these ten, but ten makes a good starting point. Keep in mind that if you want your cross-promotion to be successful, the merchants you select for your list should provide you with the following four controls:

1. A significant weekly customer count (numerical control)
2. A customer base you also want as your customers (demographic control)

3. A location that makes sense for your promotion (geographic control)
4. A combination of all of the above (Synergistic control).

With your list of ten good potential promotional partners, you're ready to present your idea just as soon as one of the owners or managers visits your business.

The Ten Steps for Setting Up a Cross-Promotion

Step #1: *Greet the merchant.* For the first ten cross-promotions you do, you'll already know the person in charge. Keep your greeting low key. You don't want to come off like a high-pressure salesperson.

Step #2: *Show a real sample.* It is extremely important to use actual samples of the pieces you want to distribute rather than machine copies or a rough draft you've scratched on a yellow legal pad. The finished piece seems to lend a stamp of approval to the promotion since the piece demonstrates that you and someone else have already done a promotion. With your first promotion, you won't have a finished sample, so be sure to print extra copies of this first promotion so you can make your future efforts easier.

Step #3: *Present the "You" benefits.* Position your piece as a nice "surprise" for the merchant's customers when they've paid their bill. It will give him or her an opportunity to show appreciation for the customer's business. (You'll learn more about this step later in this chapter.)

Step #4: *Agree on a date of distribution.* Plan on distribution for one week, two at the most. After two weeks, cross-promotion partners often loose interest in the program. Once you know when the distribution will begin and end you can figure out the expiration date for your offer. Be sure to factor the expiration date from the last day of distribution. Typical expiration dates are thirty days.

With your first promotions, give yourself plenty of time to set up your printed pieces. After the first one you can use the same format and most of the type for future ones, but the first one will take longer. Give yourself at least two to three weeks to get the pieces ready for distribution.

Step #5: *Get the weekly customer count.* You need to know how many special certificates to print. Ask questions to get an accurate number because many merchants have a tendency to inflate their customer counts. If your distribution period is for two weeks, be sure to double the weekly customer count when you visit your printer.

Step #6: *Get a copy of your partner's logo.* It's best to get a black impression on a white background if possible. If you're printing your pieces two-up, get two copies of the logo. This saves times and money in the setup. Also, if the merchant wants his or her signature to appear on the piece, collect several copies of his or her signature made with a *black* felt tip or ballpoint pen (don't use blue; it won't reproduce properly when printed), in different sizes.

Step #7: *Offer a free gift or gift certificate.* Give the merchant a small token of appreciation, a gift or gift certificate worth $5. This is not a bribe but rather a way of cementing the relationship.

Step #8: *Ask for the number of employees.* Explain that you realize bag-stuffing or distributing certificates is a little extra effort for the employees, so you want to provide value cards for all the employees. (Value cards are explained later in this chapter.) Be sure to give the employees a value card that is worth more than your certificate offer. The value card is an important step. It's often the *"glue"* that holds the promotion together and ensures that you get thorough distribution.

Step #9: *Go to your printer.* Be sure to print extra copies because you will need them when setting up future cross-promotions. (Also, send a couple of them to us at Streetfighter Marketing, 467 Waterbury Court, Gahanna, OH 43230. Fax 614/337-2233. We would be happy to do a brief, FREE, analysis for you!)

You can make these promotional pieces any size you wish, but keep in mind that the most efficient way to print at your quick printer is by using black ink on 20-pound, 8 1/2" x 11" colored paper stock. A finished piece that is 5 1/2" x 8 1/2" can be printed "two-up." If you need ten thousand certificates, for example, you print five thousand sheets of paper with two pieces printed side by side on the same page. The printer than cuts the pages in half and your print run is reduced greatly. Three to a sheet (three-up) and four to a sheet (four-up) are also common sizes.

Generally, the larger size (5 1/2 x 8 1/2) is more likely to attract the customer's attention when added to his or her bag. Three-up is a great size for an envelope stuffer. You will also want to use a different paper colors from one promotion to the next. Different colors for different promotions make it easier for your employees to keep them separate for tracking purposes.

Be sure you include the proper disclaimers in all of your certificates to avoid miscommunication to and problems with your customers. This sample disclaimer makes a good model:

This special Thank-You Certificate is good for (amount of value) savings on the *regular price* of (the item). Cannot be combined with any other special offer. Only one special "Thank-You" per visit per purchase. Cash value 1/20th of one cent. Good only at (location). Offer expires on (date).

Step #10: *Keep everyone informed.* Display samples of the pieces so that your employees know what to look for. It's sad when a new customer visits your business for the first time because of a cross-promotion piece and then leaves dissatisfied because your employee was ignorant of the promotion. There's no point in attracting new customers if you're just going to send them away angry.

Also, if your business has other stores, tell the employees in those stores about your promotion warn them that customers might be coming in to redeem the certificates. If there are other franchised outlets like the one you own in your area, you may want to give them a courtesy phone call to tell them about your promotion. They may choose to honor your offer, and then will call you in the future when they do a similar program.

Setting Up a Cross-Promotion in Person

This section offers a kind of script that you could follow when setting up a cross-promotion. The script is only intended as a guide: you should follow the basic outline but make your points in your own words so that the conversation is relaxed and very low-key. Keep in mind that this entire process, once you meet with the decision maker, should only take two or three minutes. This version is for a business owner or manager who is on your "hit list" who comes to your business as a customer.

The Introduction

You: "Hi, Mr. Jones, it's good see you again. I wonder if I could pick your brain for a minute? I've got this idea here that I thought was pretty interesting and I hoped you might like to see it. (Hand him or her your cross-promotion sample.) Here's how it works. I would like to offer you the opportunity of providing your customers with a way they can get more for their money . . . kind of a special way you can say 'Thank you!' for shopping at your store. What do you think?" (At this point, you wait for his question about the cost, which will come up about 99 percent of the time.)

Mr. Jones: "Well, it sounds pretty good, but how much does it cost?"

You: "Well, let me ask you a question. If it were free, would you do it?"

Mr. Jones: "Free? Well, yeah, sure, why not?" (The Mr. Joneses of the world usually respond with an answer like this.)

You: "Fair enough."

At this point, you have approval, but you're not finished yet. You need to take care of some details. Get the weekly customer count (if it's the type of business whose regular customers come in weekly).

You: "How many customers do you run through your store in a week?"

Mr. Jones: "Oh, about ten thousand."

You: "Great. By the way, have you tried our new hot apple brown Betty yet? It's one of my favorites."

Mr. Jones: "No, I haven't."

You: "Well, I'll tell you what. Let me bring you one with my compliments. I'm really excited about working with you on this program. Would you like to try a free one today or could I give you a card for a free one on your next visit with us? Oh, by the way, I need a good copy of your logo, preferably black on white, if you have it. We could even take it right off of your business card."

Mr. Jones: "No problem."

You: "Perfect. Oh, how would you like your name to appear on the special 'Thank You' Certificate?"

Mr. Jones: "Ah, that's John Jones, Owner."

You: "Great. Would you like your signature on there too? Your customers might really like that."

Mr. Jones: "Sure, why not."

You: (Set up the time.) "Let's see. Today is the 10th, so how about if I get your ten thousand special 'Thank-You's' to you by the 25th and you hand one to each of your customers from the 26th through the 31st?"

Mr. Jones: "No problem."

You: "By the way, how many employees do you have?"

Mr. Jones: "There are twenty-seven in all."

You: "Well, I realize that it's a little more effort for them to personally bag stuff these special certificates for each of your customers. Obviously we just can't have a stack of these sitting on the counter. So, when I return with your ten thousand special 'Thank-You's,' I'll also bring twenty-seven "Two-for-One Desert Certificates for your employees.

Mr. Jones: "Great! Thanks!"

You: "Hey, it was really nice talking you, and I'll see you on the 25th."

When the Manager Has to Get Permission from the Boss

Sometimes you might be dealing with a manager who can make a decision about things that are free, but who still wants to get permission from his or her boss. When this happens, your chances of getting permission to run this promotion lessen greatly because now you have to rely on someone else to explain the idea on your behalf, and—of course—he or she will never do it as well as you can. But there is a way to bring them around a reluctant manager without having to wait for permission from the boss.

After a manager has asked you "How much does it cost?" and you have answered, "If it were free, would you do it?" the manager might say something like, "Sure, but I have to talk to my boss first."

At that point, you need to ask two questions.

YOU: "I can certainly understand that you want your boss to be aware of this great opportunity. Let me ask you this, other than getting permission from your boss, is there any other reason why you wouldn't be able to give me the 'go-ahead' right now? (Usually there isn't.) "Well, is there any reason why you think your boss wouldn't want to do it?"

MR. JONES: "No, but I really need to get his permission before I can do anything like this."

YOU: "Oh, I totally agree. Let me suggest this. Why don't we get the ball rolling now, and, in the meantime, you get hold of your boss. If there's any problem at all, just give me a call. Fair enough?"

This technique will help in about half of these types of situations. Once the manager has made the commitment, usually he or she decides it's not even necessary to seek permission. And if he or she still does go to the boss for permission, at least he or she will make a good effort to sell the promotion for you since a commitment has been made to you. Once you get agreement, continue on as you would normally do by finding out the customer count.

If you don't get agreement, setup a time by which the manager will have a decision, then follow up. You might want to get a copy of the logo at this time, so you can follow up by phone. If you eventually get approval, this will save you another trip to the store.

Turndowns

Try to get the most out of each effort. Just as there are ways of dealing with those managers who won't make a commitment until they talk it over with their boss, there is also a way to begin to turn around a turndown.

If a potential cross-promotion partner decides not to use your cross-promotion, thank him or her, and then hand that person a low-discount coupon for your business. Tell him or her that if he or she is ever in the market for your product or service, you would like to be considered.

Though you may not have reached a few hundred or a few thousand potential customers, at least you might secure one. Then, when that manager comes into your store, you will have one more chance to convert him or her into a cross-promotion partner.

Setting Up a Cross-Promotion Appointment by Telephone

To get things moving a little faster, you don't have to wait for your ten merchants to show up. You can give them a call on the phone and invite them to your business. After all, they did participate in your free drawing. You can tell each one that he or she won second prize. Your phone conversation would go something like this:

You: (To the secretary.) "John Smith, please. (Smith picks up his phone.) John, this is Jeff Slutsky. I'm the manager of Jeff's Store down the block from you. Remember me?"

Mr. Smith: Sure do.

Let's say you've tried to call the personnel director of a major company a number of times to set up a value-card promotion, and each time the secretary tells you that the person you want is tied up and takes your message. After three attempts, use the following tactic:

You: "Great. Mr. Smith, I just pulled your business card out of our fishbowl and you've won a free (item). By the way, I came across an idea that helps provide customers more value for their money and I was wondering if I could get a little input on it when you come in to pick up your free (item)."

MR. SMITH: I guess I could come in today or tomorrow.

YOU: "Super. Well let me suggest this. Why don't we set up a time when you can come in to get your (item), then we could get together for a couple of minutes for your feedback. Okay?"

MR. SMITH: Sure

YOU: "Great. What's a good time for you in the next few days?"

MR. SMITH: Tomorrow, 1:00?

YOU: "No problem. See you then."

YOU: "Please tell Mr. Smith that his name was selected in our free drawing and that he won a free (item) at Jeff's Store. I need him to call me personally to verify and then we can set up a special time for him to pick it up."

FILTER: "Well, can't I do that for him?"

YOU: "I wish you could, but the contest rules are very specific and we must follow them or we could get into trouble. I'm sure you can understand that."

FILTER: "Sure."

YOU: "Well, see that he gets the message and make sure that he calls me within two days or we'll have to draw another name. Okay?"

FILTER: "I sure will."

YOU: "Thanks . . . Bye."

Getting Past Secretaries

Sometimes when using the phone you have to deal with a secretary or assistant first before getting to the owner or manager. I call these people "filters." They are dangerous because they can't say "Yes," but they can say "No". Usually they'll tell you, after you explain your cross-promotion idea, that their boss wouldn't be interested.

A good rule of thumb is to not explain the program to anyone but the decision maker . . . and *never* to explain it to anyone on the phone. To bypass a filter, you could use the free-drawing-winner approach.

When he calls back, you inform him that his business card was selected out of the fishbowl drawing and set up you an appointment just as you did on the phone-call approach previously suggested.

Choosing the Right Words to Sell Your Cross-Promotion

Words to Avoid When Setting Up Your Promotions

You might have noticed that I avoided using certain words that are usually associated with these types of promotions. I have found that I got a better response from a potential cross-promotion partner if I didn't use them. The words to avoid are:

Coupon: Coupons are too widely used. They're found in newspapers and they're nothing special.

Discount: Discounts will get a consumer's attention but when you mention them to a merchant they often get nervous. They may start to fear that their profit margins will get squeezed.

Advertising: Advertising is a necessary evil for most merchants. They don't like spending money on it. They don't understand it and they don't like the people who sell it. For the same reason, avoid using the words *promotion* and *marketing*.

Words to Employ When Setting Up Your Promotions

The words that have a positive effect on potential partners include:

Certificate: Certificate excites a special feeling. It's often associated with the phrase "gift certificate" which is a very positive and valued thing.

Savings: Instead of saying a "$2 Discount," say a "$2 Savings." "Save" is a very strong word. Another positive word to use instead of discount is *value*.

Benefit: "Benefit" is a much stronger word than "advertising," "marketing," or "promotion". When talking to a potential partner you can refer to your promotion as a *customer benefit program*.

Tracking Your Results

The last step in any promotion is to track the results. You need to know which ones work and which ones don't work. Since you're getting an actual printed piece back, the tracking should be very easy. But you also want to know more than those pieces of paper will tell you. The most important information you want to know from that customer is whether that customer is new or a repeat customer.

If five hundred certificates are redeemed for an offer of $2 off the regular price of $10, you've just generated $4,000 in sales, and discounted $1,000. Was this promotion successful? It depends on how many of the five hundred customers were new customers. If each customer using that certificate was already your customer and would have been likely to make the purchase at the $10 price without the certificate, that promotion was a failure because it cost you $1,000 out of your pocket.

But if out of the those five hundred redemptions, you got one hundred new customers you generated $800 of new sales that you would not have gotten. At the same time you discounted four hundred regular customers a total of $800. Most businesspeople would agree that this promotion was a success even though the actual promotion generated no increased dollars. Since you've attracted one hundred new customers from the promotion, you now have an opportunity of getting them back as regular customers.

Even if only 25 percent become regular customers, you'll find that the promotion was a tremendous success. Those twenty-five people may come back an average of once a week and spend $10 each time. That would be an additional $13,000 in sales over the next year. Moreover, if only ten of those new customers told a friend about your great service, good quality, and fair pricing, and each of those friends came to your store, you could generate another $5,200 in referral sales over the next year.

Using this kind of analysis, a promotion could be considered a long-term success when it provides you with at least several new customers. Remember, it's OK to discount regular customers during these promotions, but your primary goal is to generate new customers. To gage success, balance the new customers generated against the cost of discounts given to your regular customers.

New Product or Service Introductions

The same concept would hold true if you're using your cross-promotion to introduce a new product or service. In this circumstance, discounting your regular customers is not an issue since your goal is to get them to try something new. However, to gage success, the new product or service, when discounted to regular customers, should be something that is an add-on item that increases the total purchase. If it merely causes your customer to switch from one item to another (assuming both items are equally profitable), there is no gain.

How to Determine if the Customer Is New

Simply ask. When a customer redeems the certificate, and if you don't know from sight if that customer is a regular, simply ask nicely, "First time in our store?" Then place a "N" for new or an "R" for regular on the certificate. It's important to get your employees to do this final step because it provides you with very important information.

If a given cross-promotion is very successful, you may want to do it again. Generally two to three times a year is the most you should cross-promote with any one partner. If you do it too often, you begin to give your partner's customers too many repetitive certificates and the promotion will begin to loose its credibility.

If a given promotion results in a poor redemption rate, you will want to try to figure out the reason. Some questions you will want to ask include:

1. Were the pieces distributed properly? If the partner left them out on the counter instead of handing them out, bag stuffing them, or attaching them to invoices, the pieces loose their impact.
2. How strong was your offer? A weak offer it a waste of time. Your purpose is to get people in your store for the first time, so make sure your offer is one that will motivate a first-time buyer to visit or call you. A deep discount on an unpopular item or service is equally worthless.
3. Did you get synergistic control? Did the merchant have enough customers to make it worth your while? Was the location con-

venient enough? Were your partner's customers right for you demographically?

4. Was there a seasonality problem? Some strong cross-promotion partners, for example, a florist, a card shop, a candy shop, or a jewelry store, have specific times during the year when their customer counts swell. Promoting with an H & R Block in November will yield a much different response than a similar promotion held in early April.

If a promotion had a tremendous redemption rate but produced little or no new customers for you, you may want to ask if the promotional partner was located too close to you. Consider the plight of an oil-change place located next to a Dairy Queen. As a cross-promotion the Dairy Queen handed certificates for $2 off an oil change, while Dairy Queen's marquee promised the Peanut Buster Parfait® for just 99¢. While customers at the oil-change place were waiting for their turn, they went next door to get a Peanut Buster Parfait for 99¢. As soon as they made that purchase they received their certificate for $2 off the price of an oil change, which they took back to the oil-change place and used. The manager of the oil-change place didn't get a single new customer from the promotion and it cost him lost revenue from unnecessary discounts.

That's not to say you should never cross-promote with a business right nextdoor. In Indianapolis a Subway a few doors down from a TCBY Yogurt in the same shopping center carried out a very successful cross-promotion. Both businesses were new. They each handed out certificates for the other (see Figure 3–1) and generated lots of new customers.

If the problem is one that cannot be corrected, avoid working with that partner in the future. Discovering which partners are good for you and which are not is a very important part of the overall success of your Streetfighter Marketing program. It's likely that out of forty promotions your first year, ten or fifteen will be unsuccessful. That's part of the learning curve. Most of those will be in the first three to six months. Yet you'll find that the number of your unsuccessful promotions drops dramatically as you continue with your program.

FIGURE 3–1

This promotion generated new customers even though they were located very close to each other.

Chapter Summary

To save time and get better results, start with a business-card drawing to find out which of your existing customers would make good promotional partners. Then you can set up your first promotions when those customers visit to your business. Also take drives through your neighborhood to discover all the potential promotional partners that do business there.

Always stress the benefits of these promotions from the promotional partner's point of view. Set it up as an "added value" and a way for the partner to personally think her or his customers.

Print your promotional pieces at your local quick printer using black ink and colored 20-pound paper. Print your pieces two, three, or four to sheet of paper to keep printing costs to a minimum. If you own a business that targets the affluent, you may want to use higher quality piece with multiple colors, raised print, and textured paper.

Be sure to track the results of each promotion you do. You especially want to knew how many of your redemption certificates brought in *new* customers as opposed to regular customers who might have paid full price.

Analyze each promotion you do, especially the unsuccessful ones, so you can learn from each one and get increased results from the next promotions. You want constant improvement.

4

How to Get More Cooperation from Other Area Businesses

Up to this point we have only explored retail merchant certificates as the first of the ten ways to get free distribution of your promotional messages. In this chapter you'll read about how some variations of cross-promotions help you get distribution through four more channels:

1. Major employers
2. Associations and organizations
3. Educational institutions
4. Businesses and organizations that serve businesses

In addition you'll read about the Streetfighter approach to special situations including:

1. Reaching people who have recently moved into the neighborhood without paying for it
2. Getting double or triple the distribution by joining forces with other noncompetitive merchants
3. Getting other merchants to provide you with value-added or free premiums for *your* customers
4. Getting your competitors to work with you!

Value Cards

A value card is a cross-promotion variation, one different from the merchant certificate in that the offer provided to the recipient can be used repeatedly. A one-time offer should usually be preferred to a repetitive offer because once you've motivated new customers to visit with you, you want them to come back to your store because of the service and quality product you offer, not because of the discount. However, major employers, organizations, and educational institutions rarely cooperate with that type of promotion. Other terms for value-card promotions include VIP cards and discount cards. As I mentioned in Chapter 2, you may get a better response from potential partners by avoiding use of the word "discount."

These programs are most effective when you set an expiration date for the value card. Ideally a limit of thirty days would be great, but there are instances, where, in order to gain the acceptance of the promotional partner, you have to give them sixty to ninety days of value. In one instance, where the partner was a teacher's union for the state of Indiana, the term required was the entire school year (see Figure 4–1). The same might apply with a bowling or softball league. Remember: the main goal of these promotions is to introduce new customers to your business. By providing those customers a value for a lengthy time, you run the risk of having them visit you only so long as they get that special offer. In this one respect, the value card has a slight disadvantage over the merchant promotion. Instead of being a one-time offer, the value card is used repeatedly until the expiration of the card. So you want to make sure that you think through your offer very carefully. Since a customer can use it repeatedly, the offer should usually be less than what you offer on a one-time merchant certificate.

But this downside is minor compared to a major potential benefit: big employers and schools can provide you with many customers. In Delaware, Ohio, a McDonald's did some heavy-duty Streetfighting. There were fifteen major employers in that small community. Within three months the McDonald's set up a value-card promotion with fourteen of those fifteen major employers, and also established a number of other community promotions (see Figure 4–2).

In Seattle there was a Minit-Lube located just a mile down the road from a John Deere distribution center. The new personnel director at John Deere was waiting for his car. He was approached by the Minit-Lube manager, who offered him a cross-promotion. The entire promotion was set up in a few minutes. In this instance the

FIGURE 4–1

This promotion went statewide and ISTA did the printing.

**Indiana
State
Teachers
Association**

Dear I.S.T.A. Member:

Through a special arrangement with the Indiana Pizza Hut® restaurants, we have secured for our membership the attached 10% Discount Card.

Your card entitles you to 10% Off the regular menu price of any Pizza Hut® food purchase, at any of the participating Indiana Pizza Hut® restaurants listed on the reverse side of this card.

Make note that this is **not** a one-time discount. Retain your card. Use it anytime and everytime you visit Pizza Hut®.

In addition, some Pizza Hut restaurants offer special store tours for student groups, Birthday or Party accomodations and ideas for school fund-raising projects. Contact your Home Town Pizza Hut manager for details.

Sincerely,

Robert G. Barcus

Robert G. Barcus
Assistant Executive Director,
Special Services

 DISCOUNT CARD

Indiana State Teachers Association

The bearer of this card is a member of Indiana State Teachers Association and is entitled to a TEN PERCENT discount off the **regular menu price** of any food item at participating Indiana Pizza Hut® restaurants.
Retain this card and use it everytime you visit us through June 1, 1982.

DINE IN OR CARRYOUT

Offer good at participating
Pizza Hut® restaurants
in these Indiana communities.

Anderson	LaGrange
Attica	La Porte
Auburn	Lawrenceburg
Bedford	Lebanon
Bloomington	Logansport
Bluffton	Lowell
Brazil	Madison
Brownsburg	Marion
	Martinsville
Charlestown	Merrillville
Chesterfield	Michigan City
Chesterton	Mishawaka
Clarksville	Monticello
Columbus	Mooresville
Connersville	Muncie
Corydon	
Crawfordsville	Nappanee
Crown Point	New Albany
	New Castle
Danville	New Haven
Decatur	Noblesville
Delphi	North Manchester
De Motte	
	Paoli
Elkhart	Peru
Elwood	Plymouth
Evansville	Portage
Fort Wayne	Princeton
Frankfort	
Franklin	Rensselaer
	Richmond
Gary	Rochester
Goshen	Rockville
Greencastle	
Greenfield	Schererville
Greensburg	Scottsburg
	Seymour
Hammond	South Bend
Highland	
Hobart	Terre Haute
	Tipton
Indianapolis	
Jeffersonville	Valparaiso
	Vincennes
Kendallville	
Knox	Wabash
Kokomo	Warsaw
	Winchester
Lafayette	

Signature of Member

• Valid only when signed, and Non-Transferable.

• Discount not applicable to Alcoholic Beverages or Indiana Sales Tax.

• We reserve the right to ask for corresponding ISTA membership identification.

• Not good in conjunction with other coupons, discounts or special offers.

personnel director had the authority to approve value-cards distribution to all the employees, but didn't have the authority to grant use of the company logo. No problem: the Minit Lube manager just typeset the name. It wasn't worth the effort to get permission for the logo (see Figure 4–3).

Sometimes you may run into a less-than-cooperative personnel director. Then you must look for alternative ways to infiltrate the

FIGURE 4–2

Fourteen of the fifteen major employers did a value card.

WHITESIDE MANUFACTURING CO.

Whiteside

Dear Employee:

Recently, we arranged with McDonalds® of Delaware on 279 S. Sandusky for you to get your own McDonald's Special Value Card.

With this special card you will receive one free Large Order of French Fries with the purchase of any large sandwich*. Simply detach the card below and present it at the time of purchase.

Your Special Value Card can be used over and over again for as long as indicated by the expiration date below. Please note this special arrangement is not valid with any other special or coupon and subject to the terms and conditions stated below on your card.

Your Special Value Card is provided specifically for your use only. McDonald's reserves the right to ask for identification to prove your affiliation with us.

We're very pleased to provide you this extra benefit, so feel free to start using it right away. And remember, "It's A Good Time, For The Great Taste® , of McDonald's!".

*(Big Mac® Sandwich, †Quarter Pounder, or †Quarter Pounder with Cheese Sandwich, (†weight before cooking 113.4 gms.), Chicken McNuggets® , or McD.L.T.® .)
©1986 McDonald's's Corporation

- -

M McDonald's™   **GR**
VALUE CARD
The bearer of this card is affiliated with:

WHITESIDE MANUFACTURING

and is entitled to one **FREE LARGE ORDER OF FRENCH FRIES** with the purchase of any large sandwich* at the regular price. Valid only at McDonald's® at 279 S. Sandusky, Delaware Ohio. Show your card at time of purchase. Expires: 7/30/86
Not valid with any other offer. Limit one card per person per purchase. Cash value 1/20th of 1¢.
*(Big Mac® Sandwich, †Quarter Pounder, or †Quarter Pounder with Cheese Sandwich, (†weight before cooking 113.4 gms.), Chicken McNuggets® , or McD.L.T.® .)
©1986 McDonald's's Corporation

---

same group. The 20th-Century Automotive company wanted to get its discount cards out to all the employees of a nearby factory. The executives at the plant wouldn't bite. So 20th-Century then approached the head of the local United Auto Workers (UAW). He saw this opportunity as an extra benefit that they could provide to his union members at no cost to them. A total of ten thousand value cards were mailed by the UAW to their area members. That one promotion doubled 20th-Century's business (see Figure 4–4).

FIGURE 4–3

This promotion was set up in the waiting room.

JOHN DEERE COMPANY

Dear Employee:

Recently, we arranged with the Minit-Lube® located at:

521 N.E. 181st, Portland, Oregon

for you to get your own special Minit-Lube Value Card. With your Special Value Card you will save $2.00 on the regular price of full service lubrication featuring Quaker State products. Simply detach the card below and present it at the time of purchase.

Your Special Value Card can be used over and over again for as long as indicated by the expiration date below. Please note that special arrangement is not valid in combination with any other offer and subject to the terms and conditions stated on your card.

Your Special Value Card is provided specifically for your use only. Minit-Lube reserves the right to ask for identification to prove your affiliation with us.

We're very pleased to provide you this extra benefit so feel free to start using it right away. And remember to "look for the Stripes™".

QUAKER STATE
minit-lube
®

QUAKER STATE MOTOR OIL

We feature Quaker State products

VALUE CARD

the bearer of this card is affiliated with:

JOHN DEERE COMPANY

and is entitled to a $2 savings on the regular price of the full service lubrication. Valid only at:

521 N.E. 181st, Portland, Oregon

Not valid in combination with any other offer. Limit one card per person per visit.

No Appointment Necessary.   **Expires: 1/31/87**

If you get turned down by the management of an entire company, go back and try to get a foot in the door by winning approval from a department. Such was the case in Seattle when the local Minit Lube was turned down by the local office of the Federal Aviation Association (FAA) which had one thousand employees. But one of the employees at Minit Lube had a father who was a department head at the FAA, overseeing about one hundred employees.

FIGURE 4–4

This promotion doubled business.

Fort Wayne
PUBLIC
TRANSPORTATION
CORPORATION

DEAR EMPLOYEE:

We recently arranged with 20th Century Automotive for complimentary 10% discount cards for all our employees.

With this card you will receive a 10% discount on all labor or repair work on any vehicle you own.

This card may be used over and over again for as long as indicated by the expiration date of the card. Please note that the discount does not apply to parts or sublet work.

20th Century Automotive has the latest in computer diagnostic equipment and the most skilled automotive technicians in the area, specializing in both foreign and domestic cars.

To schedule your appointment call 432-5325.

20th Century Automotive

1001 Leesburg Road • Fort Wayne, Indiana
"If we can't fix it, it can't be fixed!"
DISCOUNT CARD
The bearer of this card is affiliated with

Fort Wayne
PUBLIC
TRANSPORTATION
CORPORATION

and is entitled to a 10% discount on all Labor on automotive repair. Does not apply to parts.

Call for an appointment 432-5325.

Expires September 30, 1982

So Minit Lube managed to go through this department head to set up the promotion for his employees. Soon other employees at the FAA started asking personnel how they could get the value cards. Not long thereafter the Minit Lube District Office received a call asking what the FAA could do to get value cards for the rest of its employees.

At this point Minit Lube was in the driver's seat, so the district manager asked, "How much of a budget have you set aside for these types of employee benefit programs?" They settled for the price of the printing.

There have even been situations in which the business was able to *sell* its value cards to a major employer. That takes a very good salesperson and signifies truly advanced Streetfighting. I do not recommend this strategy because you don't want to loose sight of your main goal: get free distribution for your advertising message.

Tim Petre, a Pizza Hut unit manager in Cincinnati, was approached by a person from the Fidelity Investments office nearby to make arrangements to order pizzas for meetings and have them billed to a different address. After making the special billing arrangement and getting several small orders, Petre approached Fidelity about providing their 250 employees with value cards. The Fidelity representative was enthusiastic about the value cards and the very next day called up and ordered forty large pizzas. Moral: The effort of getting into a community by itself generates business.

Petre conducted a total of four promotions, including this one, over a one-month period. His total sales increased every week and for the month showed an increase for nearly 20 percent.

The 12-in-1 Value Card

One variation of the value card is the "12-in-1" which has a more narrow use, yet can really be effective. This promotion is usually reserved for organizations or businesses who serve businesses. This business-to-business approach gives you a very special advantage in that you get twelve times the normal distribution of the standard value card.

Instead of receiving a single value card, each business owner or manager gets an $8^{1}/_{2}$ x 11 sheet of twelve cards, printed on heavier colored stock. Suppose the local Chamber of Commerce has one thousand members. If the Chamber of Commerce mailed out one sheet to each of its members, the value-card promotion would yield one thousand cards distributed. But with the "12-in-1" approach, each member would receive a sheet of twelve cards. They then would write or type the name of their own business on each of the twelve cards, cut them up, and hand them out, keeping one for personal use. You could even add a note on the "12-in-1" sheet inviting

FIGURE 4–5

This 12-in-1 went out to all the Chamber of Commerce members, who then gave them to their employees. It got twelve times the exposure.

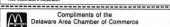

Compliments of the
Delaware Area Chamber of Commerce

VALUE CARD

The bearer of this card is affiliated with:

and is entitled to one **FREE LARGE ORDER OF FRENCH FRIES** with the purchase of any large sandwich* at the regular price. Valid only at **McDonald's® of Delaware, 279 S. Sandusky or 2091 US 23 North. Show your card at time of purchase. Expires: 6/30/86**

Not valid with any other offer. Limit one card per person per purchase. Cash value 1/20th of 1¢. *(Big Mac® Sandwich, †Quarter Pounder, or †Quarter Pounder with Cheese Sandwich, (†weight before cooking 113.4 gms.), Chicken McNuggets® , or McD.L.T.® .) · 1986 McDonald's Corporation businesses to contact the Chamber of Commerce if they want more cards. Under the system, one thousand sheets would ultimately lead to distribution of twelve thousand cards (see Figure 4–5).

The message to the Chamber of Commerce members should say something like, "Here's an employee benefit program that won't cost you a cent." If you can get the head of your Chamber of Commerce to endorse your "12-in-1" sheet, you will give the promotion increased integrity and also transfer responsibility for the discount.

Your local Chamber of Commerce is an ideal place to start. Be aware, however, that if you can get the Chamber of Commerce to go along with your promotion, it will be the first and last time it will do it. The reason? As soon as *your* sheets get distributed, all the *other* members will want to do the same thing. So the Chamber of Commerce will invariably create a policy not to ever do it again. Thus, not only do you get the promotion by being first, but you also preempt any of your competitors from ever doing anything like it. The smaller the local Chamber of Commerce, the easier it is to set up a "12-in-1" promotion.

But Chambers of Commerce aren't the only point of distribution. You could use a similar system with any business that serves other businesses. Printers, office machines companies, office supply companies, office furniture companies, telecommunication companies, paging and message services companies, business insurance companies and so on, are all excellent targets. Any company that sells to you must sell to other businesses, and therefore could serve as a conduit for masses of free advertising.

Setting Up the Value Card

Back to The Fish Bowl

Refer to your business-card drawing to discover if you have any owners, managers, CEOs, CFOs, COOs, presidents, vice-presidents, human resources managers, or personnel directors who are already your customers. Examine your drive-by notes to identify the key operations in your community that you might want to work with, and then compare the notes to the business cards to see which match up.

Once you've selected your "hit-list" of people you want to talk to, set up your value cards in much the same way as you set up your retail merchant certificates, but make several minor changes:

1. Change the presentation of the "you" benefits to reflect the new situation. Instead of offering your promotional business partner's "customers" a value-added, now you want to provide your partner's "employees, members, or students" some benefit.
2. Instead of asking for a customer count, ask for the employee, membership, or enrollment count.
3. You might want to find out the number of employees in the department so you can bring them all back something special.
4. Confirm the method of distribution so each person gets a value card.

Ensuring Proper Distribution

One challenge to setting up these types of "benefit" programs is that a personnel director might say that he'll be happy to participate in your program but he refuses to pass out your cards. Instead, he wants to mention the program in the organization newsletter and wants you to let people use their company ID card. Or he wants employees to stop by the personnel office to pick up a card if they want one. If this is the situation, you don't want to do the program because it will never work. The only members of the targeted organization who will take advantage of the program are your existing customers, and you don't want to offer discounts to them if you don't have to.

To get around this objection I usually respond by saying something like this:

"As you probably know, we're an equal opportunity organization. In order for me to provide your company with this special benefit program I have to assure my supervisors that *each* employee receives one of these special benefit cards. How do you recommend we go about doing that?"

This throws the ball back in the personnel director's court, and forces her to come up with her own solution. That solution may be to insert the pieces in pay envelopes, to mail them out with the corporate newsletter, or to provide them to the foremen or supervisors for hand distribution to the workers. But if that solution doesn't allow you to get a card into everyone's hand, walk away. It's not worth it.

Some merchants have waited by a factory entrance with special cards or fliers to distribute when the workers leave. There's nothing wrong with this system except: (1) you are using your valuable time for the distribution, and (2) you lack the credibility you would have if the program was sanctioned by the company or association.

Educational institutions are also a great place for using value cards. Any kind of post–high school student body is a good potential customer base. You might try beauty schools, vocational or technical schools, junior colleges, and so on. Smaller schools are usually more cooperative than larger ones because they are willing to scramble to offer their students even little pluses.

A large college is much more difficult to infiltrate. For example, Ohio State has about fifty thousand students on its Columbus campus. Going after the entire student body by making a pitch to the administration can be tough at best and futile at worst. But any large organization is usually made up of many smaller ones. So instead of tackling the central administration of such a large college you might do better to approach a college organization like the Greek council, the dorm board, the student bookstore, the athletic department, and so on.

Each college is different, so learn what its internal groups are. If the college provides a significant portion of your business, you need to know the campus like you would any neighborhood. The special challenge for businesses that serve college markets is that the entire student body turns over every four years. Know where the opportunities lie. Buy a subscription to the student newspaper. Call the admission office and say you're interested in sending your daughter to that school and request their admissions package. If you have any students working for you, ask them about the key organizations and associations on campus.

I went to college at Indiana University in Bloomington. As a student director of the union board, I was responsible for some of the programming intended to generate increased use of the student union building. We had a network of students in all of the dorms whose job was to announce upcoming events by putting posters in each dorm bathroom above every urinal and on every stall door. We had very high readership. Knowing how to tap into an organization like that could be more powerful than a big ad budget.

Value-Card Format

You have several different types of cards from which to choose. One powerful version is the "long-form" value card. This is a vertical piece printed three-up (three to a sheet of 8 1/2 x 11 card stock). The bottom part is the size of a business card and contains the name of the promotional partner and the expiration date. The top part has an explanation of how the value card works. It can be perforated or printed with a dotted line, to facilitate separating the top portion from the bottom card, which is kept.

Once you have the master artwork done, the only thing that changes is the logo (or name) at the top, the "dear [student, employee, or member]" salutation, the company name on the card, and the expiration date. You may also want to test a few different offers.

There are also fancier versions of the value card. Cable Saver is a value-added program used by Coaxial Communications (see Figure 4–6). This project is sponsored by local cable TV companies as a means to provide added value for cable subscribers. In this respect it functions like a "reverse cross-promotion" (covered later in this chapter). The cable company gets area businesses to provide special discounts for cable subscribers who each receive a special cable-saver card. The special deals are advertised on a dedicated cable channel as well as through print advertising.

The interesting thing about this program is that the merchant can change his or her offer on a weekly basis if he or she wants to. Customers tune into the Cable Saver channel to see what special deals are available. Since potential customers have to be a cable subscribers to get the deal, the merchant's price credibility was protected. The Cable Saver card is plastic, with the subscriber's name embossed just like a credit card.

The difference here is that the Cable Saver Card was good at many different merchants. The merchants got free advertising on cable TV, and the cable company was able to increase the value of their service at no cost to it.

FIGURE 4–6

Reverse promotions created added value.

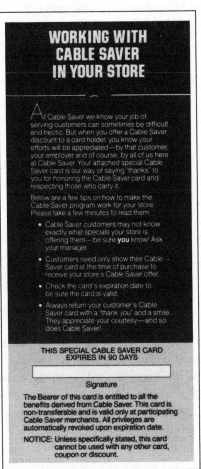

Getting Off the Wagon

At seminars I am often asked what I think of "Welcome Wagon" and other programs that deliver certificates to new households. My initial reaction is: If it works for you, use it; If it doesn't work for you, dump it. There is no right way or wrong way to advertise. The only thing that counts is results. Did it work for you?

Having said that, I must admit that I don't consider "Welcome Wagon" programs and their clones as Streetfighter Marketing because they cost real money. Moreover, your competitors can use those same programs. There may be some other services in your area that help you to reach new move-ins. But you must weigh the cost against the results to decide if such services are right for you.

You can also look for free ways to achieve the same goal of reaching new move-ins. Ask yourself, "What are the things that people do when they first move into the neighborhood?"

1. phone service
2. utilities (gas, electric, water, trash, and so on)
3. cable TV
4. home security service
5. homeowners or renters insurance
6. and so on.

All of these needs can provide you with opportunities if you know how to reach the right people at the right time with the right program.

The Two-Way Promotion

The promotions I have mentioned so far are one-way promotions: Your promotional partner hands out *your* advertising to his or her customers. The value of the certificate the partner hands out provides those customers a little more for their money at no cost to the partner. A variation of this system is the two-way promotion. In this marketing strategy, you agree to hand out each other's promotional pieces. The advantages of this strategy is that (1) it's easier to set up, and (2) you don't have to provide a value on your piece to get distribution. The disadvantage of a two-way promotion is that you're stuck with handing out the other person's promotional pieces.

Reverse Promotion

A reverse promotion is one in which you collect many certificates and use them as a value-added for your customers. This is usually done as a coupon booklet. For example, you collect eight different offers from noncompetitive businesses in your neighborhood: the car wash, the bookstore, the record shop, the movie theater, the

FIGURE 4–7

This two-way promotion traded those customers most likely to spruce up their homes.

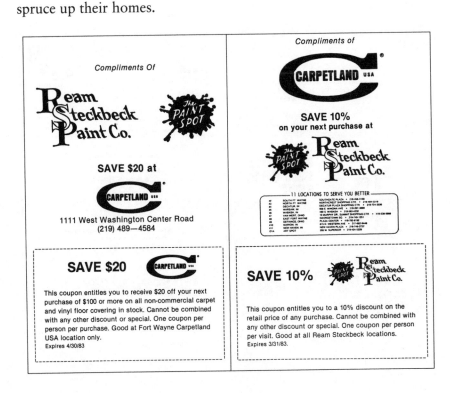

fast-food restaurant, the tire dealer, the dry cleaner, and the health club. The offers should be significant—the redemption value for this little booklet might be $25 or more if the consumer used all the certificates. This makes a nice value-added for your customers. Moreover, your eight partners in the booklet promotion now would be perfect targets for your individual certificate promotion. Thus you get a total of nine promotions in one shot (see Figure 4–8).

The reverse promotion is also used for specialty retailing. Here's an example in which the sought-after customers are those planning weddings. Instead of offering a booklet, the piece offered was a quality 5 1/2" x 4 1/4" envelope filled with engraved certificates to class-it-up a little (see Figure 4–9). Each participant in the piece—florist, bakery, caterer, photographer, travel agent,

FIGURE 4–8

This reverse promotion creates additional value each month for the customer.

limorental, printer, entertainment, tux shop, bridal shop, hair stylist, jeweler, and so on—provides a savings on some wedding-related expense.

The ideal place to distribute this packet would be when the couple buys their engagement ring. But I've seen a bridal shop use this kind of package as an incentive to commit to it. If a competitor offers a service at a lower price, you can use the "specialized reverse promotion" with total savings of $200 as a way to convince potential customers to choose your service.

We used the same technique for an apartment complex. In this situation we created a one-sheet version. The first message was from the property manager, and the other six panels were from neighborhood businesses. The value of all the certificates was about $10. A new sheet would be given to residents every month. Typical participants were the local Diary Queen, the dry cleaner, the health

FIGURE 4–9

This reverse promotion was used to help lookers commit to this store for their purchase.

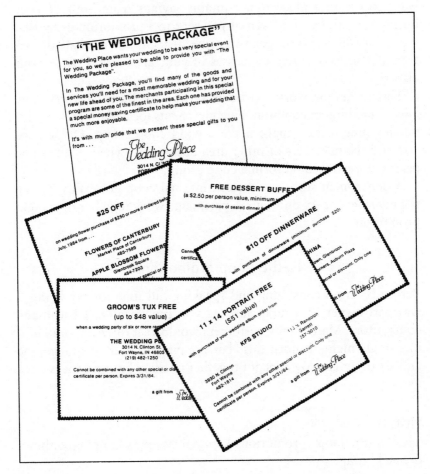

club, the auto repair shop, and so on. When a potential new resident balked at the price, this piece could be used as an incentive to increase the perceived value of the property.

Coop Promotion

This is a more advanced technique. Once you get yourself established, you may find that there are a handful of other noncompetitive business owners who are equally as creative and aggressive as you are. In this situation, it may make sense to do some cooperative promotions. In addition to a typical "two-way," you may want to create a piece that contains savings from both of your businesses, after which each of you sets up a promotion using that piece. In this way you get twice the distribution for half the effort. If you have three businesses in your group, you triple your effort.

This technique works particularly well for businesses that may have something in common. Five merchants located in the same little shopping center might make a good coop group. Or perhaps you and the managers of other area businesses owned by the same parent company could form a coop group.

A department store could form internal coop groups by having the managers of six different departments work together on a coop promotion.

In-the-Loop Promotions

Before I started consulting and speaking full time for my living, I was part-owner of a nightclub. As you can imagine, I had many competitors. Many of my customers would visit three or four clubs in a single night. To turn this "bar hopping" to our advantage, me and six other club owners got together to share business ideas once

FIGURE 4–10

This "in-the-loop" promotions kept bar hoppers hopping within a defined group.

Compliments of the United Allen County Bar Owners Association.

TWO FOR ONE

The bearer of this card is entitled to one free drink with the purchase of an identical drink at the regular price. Cannot be combined with any other discount or special. Good at:

Shenanigan's	Poor Johns
Brickly's Firehouse	The Scorpion
Grady's Place	Denny's VIP Lounge
Cagney's Pub	

---

a month. From this loose association of competitors we came up with a promotional idea to help all of us.

We knew that we had perhaps twenty-five or more direct competitors out in the marketplace. So we agreed to provide each of our customers who left any one of our seven establishments early enough to go "hopping" with a certificate for saving at any of the other six places. We thought that if we could get them to hop in the "loop of seven," we'd keep them there for the night. Even though not every club would benefit equally, all benefited enough to make it worth their effort to distribute the certificates.

Chapter Summary

Value cards are a cross-promotion variation that allow you to get free distribution of your promotional message through neighborhood major employers, associations, organizations, and educational institutions.

Value cards are set up much the same way as retail merchant certificates, but include minor changes in the presentation of the "you" benefits.

The biggest difference between the value card and the retail merchant certificate is that the value-card offer is used repeatedly for an extended time; thus a value-card offer should be set lower than the one-time savings offered in a merchant certificate.

It's critical to ensure that the promotional partner provides distribution to *each* employee, member, or student.

Other variations allow you to reach twelve times as many people per piece, to contact new move-ins to the neighborhood, to get other merchants to increase your promotional penetration, and even to get your competitors to help you.

5

Profiting from Neighborhood Nonprofits

G reat satisfaction derives from contributing to a respected non-profit agency's effort to raise money for a worthy cause. Moreover, your advertised donations can help to generate goodwill and positive publicity for your business in your community. Unfortunately, for most businesses, it has become increasingly difficult to make such charitable contributions. That's why Streetfighters take a different approach. With a Streetfighter's approach to contributing to worthy causes you can generate new customers and increased sales while becoming a local hero.

From the neighborhood-marketing standpoint, fundraising enables you to work with an entirely different group to obtain free distribution of your advertising. So far you've learned how to convince other merchants, major employers, schools, and associations to hand out various types of "invitations" to visit your business. These promotions have usually been simple, inexpensive, and not very time-consuming. Promotions with nonprofits can be just as easy or they can require much more effort; in either case, the nonprofit organization has the potential to send significant numbers of new customers to your business.

Community-involvement programs fall into three types:

1. High involvement
2. Moderate involvement
3. Low involvement

High-involvement fundraisers consume a lot of your time and cost you money. When your business pays for fundraiser advertising, for example, to promote the event, you have a high-involvement program. These types of program often provide the business with exposure, generate goodwill, but often they offer very little in the way of tangible sales and new customers. Good Streetfighters should usually stay away from these types of fundraisers. However, if you feel that your investment of both time and money will more than pay for itself eventually, a high-involvement program may be suitable for you.

Moderate-involvement fundraisers often achieve the same results as a high-involvement program, but with a fraction of the investment in time and money. Streetfighters strive to make sure that major fundraising efforts are effective, yet don't require them to use the valuable resources of their business. At the same time the donation is usually directly related to customer visits and sales. They are done once or twice a year.

Low-involvement fundraisers are ones that require almost no investment in terms of time or money. They can be used as fundraisers or to redirect a request for a donation into a promotion requiring free distribution of the business's promotional pieces. These programs can be ongoing.

Moderate-Involvement Programs

Life and Breath

Nine-year-old Valerie Yearicks suffered from cystic fibrosis and desperately needed a double lung transplant to survive. Her family and friends were doing small fundraising programs and had received some local publicity in Delaware, a suburb of Philadelphia. The general manager of an area Bob's Big Boy restaurant offered to help. The manager offered to hold a promotion in which, after accounting for his outlet's normal sales, he would donate half of the remainder of all the sales for that day to the child's charity.

Robert Yearicks, Valarie's father, spearheaded the effort to promote the event with an army of volunteers. The volunteers, some

FIGURE 5–1

These fliers were passed out by friends and family and the event increased customer counts significantly.

VALERIE YEARICKS BENEFIT
Cystic Fibrosis Awareness

148 NORTH DUPONT HIGHWAY
NEW CASTLE, DE 19720
RT. 13 ACROSS FROM
NEW CASTLE AIRPORT

104 PENN MART CENTER
NEW CASTLE, DELAWARE 19720
(302) 322-8440

Valerie is a nine year old from New Castle, Delaware and has suffered a great many of those years with cystic fibrosis. Her only hope for survival is to receive a double lung transplant. She is now waiting for a donor and will fly to Pittsburgh as soon as one is found.

How can you help Valerie?

Come to Bob's Big Boy, Rt. 13, New Castle on August 27th for a great time and great food. Proceeds from sales will go to the Valerie Yearicks Transplant Fund. There will be karate demonstrations, show cars - old and new, free University of Delaware football tickets, IBC Super Middleweight Boxing Champion Dave Tiberi, boxing tickets, many valuable door prizes and much, much more. One of these prizes could be yours.

Come out and enjoy the day and learn more about how you can help children like Valerie.

Thank you,

Parents of Valerie

Special Thanks to: Bob's Big Boy
     Korean Martial Arts Inst.
     Nu Car Chevrolet
     Marriott Corp.
     Blue Hens Football Team
     Dave Tiberi, IBC Super Middleweight Champion
     Pizza Hut
     Dunkin Donuts
     Minuteman Press

For further information about Valerie's condition, contact Pam Crouse,
A. I. DuPont Institute, (302) 651-4000.

of whom were servers at the restaurant, passed out fliers (see Figure 5–1) and put up posters that had been donated by the local quick printer. They handed out announcements door to door and placed them under windshield wipers. They got mentions in the local newspaper and on the radio. The fundraiser was also promoted for a week inside the restaurant and on the marquee, outside. For the day of the fundraiser, the restaurant's general manager arranged for karate demonstrations and an appearance by IBC Super Middleweight Champion Dave Tiberi. Door prizes and football tickets were raffled off to help the cause. The Big Boy character was out in the parking lot waving passing motorists in and drawing attention to the restaurant. The event was a huge success. A total of $2,500 was donated and Bob's Big Boy got all the credit. The restaurant manager was interviewed on two Philadelphia TV stations. The restaurant received an estimated $20,000 worth of free publicity. Customer counts were up 30 percent, and many of those were new faces.

This program took *moderate* effort on the part of the manager, but most of the promoting was done by the volunteers. The manager had no risk because he only promised to donate in excess of what his outlet would normally gross on a typical Wednesday. If the group supporting Valerie Yearickes hadn't promoted the event and sales were flat, Bob's Big Boy would have made no donation. When a donation was made, the 50 percent covered the cost of food and labor, so again there was no risk. Many new customers did visit the store and paid full price for their meals. You could spend twice as a much on standard media and not get the type of results that this type of promotion achieves.

Pulpit Power

A Super Valu grocery-store owner set up a register-tape promotion to help area churches raise money. The participating church had the responsibility of doing all the promoting to its congregation. If church members did their grocery shopping at this Super Valu, they could bring their register-tape receipts to the church, where they were deposited in a special collection bin. After the tapes were returned to the Super Valu, a percentage of their value was donated to the church. Each participating church was highly motivated to get as many of their members as possible to do the bulk of their shopping at this store. If you are the owner of one of three competing grocery stores, and they each offers basically the same products at competitive prices, a charitable motivator like this could give you a Streetfighter edge.

You Sew, and the Charity Reaps

Bob Kramer of Karmer's Sew & Vac in Cincinnati ran a promotion with the Clovernook Center, a well-known home and opportunity center for the visually handicapped, which was located around the corner from one of his stores. The Clovernook Center had asked area businesses to contribute cash to its renewal and expansion program. Kramer turned this request for a donation into a promotional opportunity and offered the Clovernook Center a cash rebate on sales it could generate. The Clovernook Center got 10 percent of sales based on the following four rules:

1. Only receipts for purchases made and services ordered at the North College Hill Kramer's Sew & Vac during the months of April, May, and June would qualify.
2. Receipts had to be turned in to the Clovernook Center.
3. Kramer's would issue a check to the Clovernook Center for 10 percent of the total net sales before tax.
4. Rebates on individual transactions would be limited to a maximum of $200.

According to Kramer, his stores got of a lot of exposure in the Clovernook Center's mailings, which included a monthly newsletter. Sew & Vac also got positive publicity in the local press, which attracted new customers and boosted sales. Goodwill was created in the immediate market area.

Healthy Gums for a Healthy Community

Dr. Steve Oppenheimer, a dentist in Atlanta, organized a teeth-cleaning event that raised money to aid hurricane victims in a neighboring state. He opened his office on Sunday and offered to donate his normal fee for teeth cleaning to the hurricane relief efforts. He promoted this event primarily to his own patients, but he encouraged them to bring their friends. In addition to attracting new patients, Dr. Oppenheimer received very good publicity, including an article in the *Atlanta Constitution*.

Making Impact Is a Convenience

Stubby's Food Marts, a six-store chain in the Houston, Texas area, does a fundraising program with the local Muscular Dystrophy Association (MDA) chapter. Stubby's generates impressive returns on a small investment through the sponsorship of car washes, shamrock sales, and other drives throughout the year, according to an article in *Convenience Store News* written by Barbara Grondin Francella. But it is Stubby's summer fundraising finale that regularly generates a lot of favorable publicity in the local media.

The summer event is a Carnival held in a large circus tent. This big fundraiser features magicians and fortune tellers. Adult's are drawn to a bake sale and a garage sale, while kids are attracted to a variety of games and a "face painter." Customers also have an opportunity to drop the local sheriff into a dunking tank and to bail local business leaders out of "jail." Recently a Houston radio station broadcast live from the event and one of the city's most popular newscasters attended as a guest.

The event raises more than $10,000 each year for MDA, including the 1 percent of the store sales Stubby's donates. "We put a few thousand dollars into the fundraiser every year, but we've gotten really well known because of it," Ryan Stubbs said. "It is good exposure for our stores and it's good for the community."

The Trade-In Donation

Kuppenheimer, a chain of discount, men's clothing stores, turns a sale into a charity event. Customers can turn in any suit they own and get a credit for the purchase of a new suit. Kuppenheimer then repairs the used suits, has them cleaned, and donates them to a local homeless shelter.

This is a "moderate-involvement" promotion because it does require some effort for repairs and cleaning (the latter is provided by the dry cleaning cosponsor). Also, Kuppenheimer has to advertise the event at its own expense. What makes this promotion nice is that Kuppenheimer requires its customers to bring in their old suits to get a savings on new suits. If Kuppenheimer made the same savings available with a coupon in the paper, the promotion would not have the same credibility or appeal.

In Columbus, Ohio, a local grocery-store chain has created a partnership with a local dry-cleaning chain. The two chains serve as collection points for used coats. Neither chain offers savings on purchases when someone donates a used coat. This is an effective promotion that benefits the needy at minimal cost to the businesses.

Trade-in promotions have also been used for collecting shoes at a shoe store, eye glasses at an optical center, books at a bookstore, canned goods at a grocery or convenience store, and toys at a toy store. And there are many more possibilities. These same items could be collected by any business that volunteers to be used as a collection sight, but your business will get more benefit if you sell a product similar to the used item collected for charity.

If you don't offer a product that lends itself to a trade-in approach, then it makes sense to volunteer your store as a collection sight for something else. It costs you nothing and you're likely to get some positive publicity and some new customers for your effort.

Low-Involvement Programs

Low-involvement programs are designed to be used on a regular basis. The serve as a kind of "on-the-shelf" community involvement and usually don't make as much impact as the moderate-involvement programs, yet they can give your image a boost while motivating new customers to visit your store and buy your product or service.

Lead Us not unto Donation

An office-equipment business turned a lead-generation program into a community-involvement program. Whenever a copy-machine technician finished repairing the machine in one office, he would stop by other offices on the floor and announce that his company was doing a special fundraising promotion. If an office agreed to fill out a one-page questionnaire about its copy-machine needs, his company would donate $2 to a specific local charity. Since the questionnaire was short and filling it out would benefit a good cause, most people were happy to fill out the questionnaire.

What was unique about this program was that this office-machine company was able to motivate *repair* people, not salespeople, to actually make cold calls to gather information that the copy-machine company could put to good use to increase its customer base. Presumably, the charitable tie-in made the task of doing these cold calls much easier for the repair people. Thanks to this clever program, the office-machine company got hundreds of leads for new clients, which their sales force followed up on, and the charity received a nice donation.

Free Use

This easy promotion is for those businesses that market durable goods, like cars, appliances, and electronic equipment, or *some* kinds of services. "Free use" means you allow a nonprofit to use your merchandise or service for its event, free of charge. By lending the nonprofit your merchandise or service, you become a major sponsor of the event without having to contribute cash.

FREE WHEEL'N

"Free-use" doesn't have to be tied to a nonprofit program. At an area Professional Golf Association (PGA) tournament a local car dealer provides a fleet of cars for the use of the participating pro golfers. Each "loaner" has a "official PGA car" message painted on its doors. The car dealership gets great exposure, and when the tournament is over it has an easy job selling the cars that pro golfers drove in because each car has a story.

WIRED

Long-distance phone companies in conjunction with a nonprofit group will often set up shop in a major mall during the Christmas season. Anyone who makes a donation of a certain size to the charity is given the opportunity to make a free five-minute call to anyone in the world to wish them season's greetings. The mall and the charity do the promoting.

KEEPING YOUR HEAD BELOW WATER

Another version of the "free use" idea was employed by a scuba-diving center on the West Coast. The center's instructors and advanced scuba students teamed up to remove underwater debris from an area river. It was a fun promotion for the participants, and garnered great publicity for the dive center, including a long article in the local paper with a photo of their effort. Promotion of the event and its accompanying publicity helped raise tremendous awareness for treating the environment with respect. Instead of raising money, the scuba center removed garbage. Its "charitable contribution" was its effort on behalf of the environment.

The Buck Stops Here

One nice low-involvement program is what I call the "buck" technique. To illustrate this technique I will use a hypothetical business, Jeff's Book Emporium, an average independent bookstore.

The local Boy Scout troop is raising money to buy new playground equipment for the park in their community. They decide to hold a raffle and offer a grand prize of a new 10-speed bike. The troop members go door to door to sell their raffle tickets. The first question that they're always asked is "How much are they?" They respond, "Each ticket costs $1 but with each one you buy you get $1 off your next purchase at Jeff's Book Emporium." (The piece actually reads $1 off the purchase of $10 or more.)

In this situation a high-visibility group is going door to door and giving people a five-second live commercial for the bookstore. When a person buys a raffle ticket he or she is handed a "book buck" good for a savings on a future book purchase. This device makes it easier for the Boy Scouts to sell their tickets since the donor gets an immediate value as well as a shot at the grand prize. The bookstore gets free distribution of the book buck, compliments of the Boy Scout troop. If the Scouts sell a thousand tickets, the bookstore owner gets a thousand pieces of advertising distributed free, while at the same time building a "good guy" image in the community.

The bucks themselves can become a self-perpetuating marketing device if they include a message like this on the front: "Jeff's Book Emporium supports a wide variety of community events. If you would like some help with your next fundraiser, call Jeff at 614/337-7474 for details." Thus a person getting one of these bucks who belongs to the Lion's Club or the Rotary may call Jeff to contribute "book bucks" for an upcoming fundraiser.

FIGURE 5–2

Three examples of "bucks" that can be used as needed.

Another valuable feature of this buck technique is that once you set it up with your quick printer, it takes very little time to order them. They're usually set up six to a sheet of paper (six-up) so they trim down to dimensions similar to a dollar bill. The only thing that changes with each promotion is the name of the nonprofit

FIGURE 5–3

This buck is printed on two sides with a generic message on one side.

group and the expiration date. The printer keeps the master "buck" on file. If B'nai B'rith is having their fundraiser, for example, you simply call your printer and tell her that you need three thousand book bucks for the B'nai B'rith with an expiration date of November 15. The printer drops in the minor copy changes, prints and trims the bucks, and has them ready for pickup by the group in no time. The nonprofit group goes to the printer to get your bucks, signs for them, and you have no other involvement.

You can call your bucks anything you want to. Some generic examples include "pizza bucks," video bucks, or community cash (see Figure 5–2 for some real-life examples). Once you develop your low-involvement buck you only use it for nonprofit groups.

Though they can be printed on one side only, many of the "bucks" are printed on both sides. One side contains the information that encourages people to contact the manager for help with their fundraisers. The other side contains the fundraising organization's name, the offer, and its expiration date (see Figure 5–3 for a sample).

If you choose to use the two-sided version, consider preprinting the generic side that never changes. As I mentioned, the typical buck is printed six to a sheet of paper. If you plan on going through four thousand bucks during the next year, for example, have your printer preprint 700 to 750 sheets of bucks. This will give you some extra sheets to cover printing mistakes. In printing, every time you go to press there is a set-up charge. The first sheet of paper is the most costly and each sheet you print in the same run becomes progressively less costly. So it's always best to print in larger quantities when it makes sense.

A two-sided run will cost you almost twice as much as a one sided run. The only thing you save in the second run is the cost of the paper. So, since you have a common side for all of your bucks, by running a year's supply at one time you save money. Have your printer store the already printed sides. Then when you need five hundred bucks for the area Jaycees, call the printer and she will run off eighty-four sheets of bucks with the generic side already printed. Your two-sided run will cost you just a little more than the one-sided run.

This same idea holds true if you print your promotional pieces in more than one color. The second color costs you nearly as much as the first color, plus an additional set-up charge. Arrange your artwork so that the material in the second color is always the same in every piece. The information in the second color might be your logo, directions to your business, or your phone number. You can preprint that portion in quantity and have the printer store it. Then use the preprinted pieces as needed.

BOOSTING THE BUCK

To begin to promote the buck's availability, you can do a simple flier mailing to the nonprofit groups in your community (see Figure 5–4 for an example). Your local Chamber of Commerce usually has a list of these groups. Add a headline to your flier, for example, "If You Have a Good Cause, We Have $25,000 of Neighborhood Support," to get their attention. Of course, the $25,000 refers to your bucks. It would also be a good idea to include, a special "Thank You Certificate" at the bottom of the flier as an additional attention-getter.

FIGURE 5–4
A flier sent to nonprofit groups gets the program going.

IF YOU'VE GOT A GOOD CAUSE . . . YOUR NEIGHBORHOOD MARATHON HAS $25,000 WORTH OF LOCAL HELP FOR:

(insert name of community, big and bold!)

THE QUALITY LUBE & OIL SERVICE.

MARA-BUCKS For:

For helping your community run a little smoother, we're going to grease your palm with a $1 savings on each $10 in service you buy at Marathon. So buy $20 save $2, $30 save $3, etc. up to $100.

Redeemable only at the location listed on the back.
Offer subject to terms and conditions on the back.

MARA-BUCKS for you! MARA-BUCKS for our community!

An American Company Serving America.

Raising funds for your neighborhood or community projects may have become increasingly difficult in recent months. If so, all of us here at your local Marathon would like to help you . . . and here's how:

It's called "**MARA-BUCKS**" and as you can see from the sample, it's good for a $1.00 savings on each $10 in service you buy at Marathon.

Whether your group is holding a Raffle, Dance, Candy Sale, Car Wash, Bazaar or other current event, giving a MARA-BUCK with every purchase seems to remarkably increase the dollars raised!

And as our way of making a contribution to our community, we've set aside $25,000 worth of MARA-BUCKS for your fund raising projects in the coming year. To find out if your group qualifies, just contact us at the phone number listed below:

(insert store address, locator,
phone
and Dealer's name)

Help for you, too!

In addition to help for your organization, we would like to offer you a special reward for helping your community. We realize that fund raising and other valuable community programs and projects are time consuming and even a lot of extra miles on your car. So, as a way of showing our appreciation for your efforts, please feel free to use the special "Thank-You" certificate and we look forward to seeing you very soon at Marathon.

An American Company Serving America.

SAVE $2

This special "Thank-You" certificate is given to you for efforts "**above and beyond**" and entitles you to a $2 savings on the regular price of your next regular oil change and lubrication at Marathon. Not combinable with any other offer. Only one special "Thank-You" per person per visit. Good only at:

(insert address,
locater, phone)

Expires:
Appointment may be necessary.

You can have the quick printer enlarge your flier to poster size. Mounted on colored artboard, the enlarged flier will make a nice display on your store wall.

Hand out copies of your flier to your customers. You can also use other signs, counter displays, window banners, buttons, and so on, to make your *own* customers aware of the bucks availability. This way, not only do you tie into nonprofit groups, but you work with your own customers to kick off the program.

The bucks program is the kind of program you do as requested. Once it's off the ground, groups call you. You may do bucks promotions several in one month and none the next. There may be times of the year when you do a number of these promotions (Even when doing many of these promotions, we still want to do other promotions too. Don't let the bucks count as your three promotions for the month.)

While most bucks are handed out free in return for a donation, sometimes a nonprofit group will actually go door to door and sell them, usual in an even-trade manner: a dollar donation for a dollar off a purchase at your business. The benefit to you is the same.

Another twist on the buck promotion is to rebate part of the revenue to the charity. Barbara Smith had a deadly disease and the local Luby's cafeteria designed a promotion to help pay for some of her medical costs. Barbara's husband, Jimmy Smith, was given 2,500 bucks (called Luby's Loot) which promised $1 off any purchase of $5 or more. Luby's promised to donate 50¢ toward Barbara's medical expenses for each buck that was redeemed.

MORE BUCKS FOR WARBUCKS

The buck idea runs into difficulty when the nonprofit group is raising money for a cause that appeals to a more affluent audience. If your business caters to an upscale, charitable causes like the art museum, performing arts groups, hospitals, and so on, will probably pull more of these kinds of customers. But to capture the attention of the affluent, you have to offer more than a "buck-off" certificate. The standard buck promotion just doesn't draw get the support of the wealthy. Perhaps they feel awkward using the bucks or fear looking cheap.

To capture this group, up the ante. For this group you use a five-

FIGURE 5–5
By using a slightly different approach, you can influence the affluent.

Over $15,000 Raised for
Al Ruble Heart Fund

On Sunday, November 16th Eagle's Nest was host to a special $100 a Plate Dinner and Charity Auction that raised over $15,000 to help pay for Al Ruble's Heart Transplant.

We are extremely proud of our contribution to this special cause and look forward to serving the Oklahoma City Community for many years to come.

Sincerely,

Brett J. Deignan

Eagle's Nest, Mgr.

---

buck or ten-buck certificate. You print the piece on a 5 1/2 x 8 1/2 foldover so that it looks more like an invitation than a buck or coupon. The face value of the piece can be donated directly to the cause, not taken off the donor's bill, so the customer pays full price.

The nonprofit group distributes the pieces to its members and promotes their use. The advantage of this approach is that the donation is redeemed only when the recipient actually makes a purchase at your fine restaurant, German-import car service, golf or tennis pro shop, jewelry store, or the like.

Telethon Triumph

Major fundraising drives are great opportunities for getting your low-involvement pieces handed out. A telethon, for example, can prompt thousands of people to pledge money. Immediately after the telethon comes the task of collecting this money. When those invoices are sent go out, you can include your piece with a message like this:

We wish to thank you in advance for your prompt response to your pledge. As a special "thank you" we're providing you with this special certificate good for (offer) at your next visit to (store or business). It's just our way of showing you how much we appreciate your support for (organization).

Free Fruit for The Fruitless

The ultimate version of trash to treasure is a program used regularly by J. King Food Distributors in Oakland, New York, a company that supplies many of the restaurants and cafeterias on Long Island. John King wants to provide his customers the absolute best in produce, so he has his people repack three hundred cases of fruits and vegetables every day to separate the highest quality produce from the rest. Less-than-perfect produce, such as an apple or cantaloupe with a bruise, or an orange with slight discoloration in the skin, is set aside. It's all perfectly edible, but not of the quality that a restaurant wants to serve.

The set-aside produce is picked up daily by the local food bank. King gets to use his food gifts as a tax-deductible donation (which includes an additional 10 percent for operating expenses). It actually costs him nothing to provide over $40,000 (wholesale) worth of food to the needy each year: if he didn't donate the food, he would have to throw it out. (When you consider that garbage removal on Long Island is $80 a ton, King probably comes out a little bit ahead.)

King receives no publicity, nor does he attract additional customers as a result of his efforts. Only a few people know about his contribution to the community, but it is a way he can help others at no cost to his business while achieving better quality for his customers.

In Cold Storage

NorthAmerican Van Lines came to the rescue for a couple dozen midwestern families who were flooded out of their homes. They offered the families the use of their unused trailers to store their belongings for a few months while they got back on their feet. They had hundreds of vacant trailers at the time. The company got national exposure for its charitable act, including a mention on network TV.

A national motel franchisee with a location on a major interstate highway provided the state police with special emergency value cards that they could give to stranded motorists. If there was an available room at the motel, it would provide a room for the night at a significant discount for emergency situations. As a result of this gesture, the state police began recommending this particular motel to motorists who asked them where they should stay for the night.

Another national hotel franchisee came to the rescue of a family who was forced out of its home because of a fire during a blizzard. The hotel provided the family with a room for a week, which was enough time for the insurance company to arrange temporary housing for the family at an apartment complex. This generous act received a great deal of local publicity and, of course, the cost of providing it was minimal.

When disaster strikes your community you can be a hero by having a promotion ready to help people in need. One way to prepare for a disaster is to ensure that you will be open during these times. Luby's cafeterias, which have some locations in Florida, have a disaster plan in place which includes letting the government emergency services and the Red Cross know that they'll be open. They volunteer their location as a collection site for clothing and canned goods. Since they're a disaster-relief site, the power company has them on its priority list for power, listed just below the hospitals and other emergency operations.

This is a great public service and provides Luby's with great exposure and goodwill during disasters. The purpose of this promotion is *not* business as usual. This is one of the few situations where you don't tie your efforts directly to sales, but you certainly will become a more successful operation for providing such an effort.

Nonprofit Streetfighters

Now let's look at community involvement from a nonprofit organization's point of view. Charity groups need to be Streetfighter marketers too. If you manage a nonprofit, you probably find that getting cash donations from businesses is becoming more and more difficult. Yet if you can help somebody's business to get more customers or to improve its profitability, you will increase the likelihood of getting his or her support dramatically. By understanding donations from the businessperson's point of view, you can design your request in such a way that the business is more than happy to contribute.

First you need to understand the difference between product-cost dollars and real dollars. It may take many dollars of sales to generate a dollar of profit. Therefore, it's much easier for a business to donate its products and services than to donate cash. Donating products and services costs a business much less, and if such donations are promoted properly, they will provide the business with community goodwill, more customers, and higher sales.

The charity auction works well for both charities and businesses. The nonprofit organization asks local businesses to donate their products and services to the auction and then promotes the event. The business gets exposure in the program book and from the attendees at the event. A business can often rid itself of quality items that aren't selling, thereby giving attendees an opportunity to pick up some bargains. Both the business donor and the person who buys the donated product are contributing to the charity.

Service businesses can participate through the donation of gift certificates. One popular offer donated by a local pizza restaurant was a pizza a month for a year. This offer had a face value of $150, but the out-of-pocket cost to the restaurant was about $50. (When the winner comes in to get his or her free pizza, he or she is likely to buy beverages, salad, and more, so the restaurant probably makes back more than it gives away.)

Don't hesitate to approach businesses to ask for their help by making their office or store the site for an event or proposing a value-added, savings, certificate, or sponsorship program. When you approach a business for help, explain to its owner how he or she will have an opportunity to get new customers and make profit while at the same time generating money for your cause.

Solicitations

Businesses frequently receive calls from telemarketers asking for cash donations. From a marketing point of view donating money to these causes does you no good. In many instances a professional fundraiser is asking for your money, and the cause receives only a small fraction of the money. You should turn these callers down. But you need to make sure the caller is a professional fundraiser first because you don't want to get a "bad guy" image in your community.

The same thing happens when people come to your place of business asking for a donation or to participate in their advertising book. You want to turn them down too, but to do so in a nice way so that you won't hurt your image. The best way is to have them call someone else, preferably out of town, who can turn them down and keep you out of it. This ploy works if you are part of a franchise or dealer network. See if someone at corporate headquarters can provide a nice "turn down" service for you. You simply tell everyone who asks for a charitable donation that those decision are made at corporate headquarters, it's out of my hands.

Chapter Summary

Keep the cause local. You'll have a much better response if the sponsoring group is from the neighborhood and is raising money that directly benefits your neighborhood. Also, support only legitimate groups and causes. Nothing could be worse for your community image than inadvertently supporting a less-than-just cause. Do a little homework before making a commitment.

Choose aggressive, motivated, well-organized groups. If they don't strongly promote the event, there's little to be gained. At the same time, avoid controversial groups and causes. If you pick a group or a cause that has polarized your community, you could anger many customers, which defeats the purpose of your participation in the group's fundraiser. There are many worthwhile fundraising opportunities that everybody in the community can support.

Take advantage of publicity opportunities. It's best to have the nonprofit group contact the media since they're likely to get a stronger response than you would. But you may have to guide them if they're not media savvy.

Choose causes with specific goals. The easier it is for the public to visualize the use for the money, the greater your chances for success. It also helps to have a specific amount of money as a target to be raised. Even if you fall short of that goal, your response should be better overall.

Use variety. Have both "minimal-involvement" programs (everyday or ongoing) and one or two "moderate-involvement" or special-event programs in your repertoire.

Start looking for a good nonprofit partner. Use your own employees and customers as resources to gain knowledge about the community's nonprofit groups and their needs.

Promotions with nonprofit groups bring in new customers who you want to develop into steady customers. Use bounce-back certificates to encourage repeat visits and free drawings to build mailing lists.

When possible, require the participants to visit your business and make a purchase. Not all community-involvement programs can be done at your place of business, but there is an obvious advantage when it can be made part of the promotion.

Have a strategy for gracefully rejecting requests for donations or converting them into programs that will help you.

6

Promoting with Events

Creating a promotional event can be a powerful way to bring customers into your business. An event creates excitement about your products and services and provides an opportunity to motivate many new buyers to visit you for the first time. A promotional event is more than a sale, though special pricing may be one element in your event. A promotional event is more like a party or a celebration. Everything about it should feel special. If you use a special price as part of your celebration, than that special price should be *very* special.

The Blow-Out Event

The blow-out event uses the most aggressive price strategy to bring customers out of the woodwork. You want to make the prices at this event so enticing that they can't afford to miss it. But low prices alone, while often a good draw, doesn't leverage this activity as much as a well-thought-out function. Calling your event a "celebration" allows you to offer special pricing or value-added without conveying the message to your customers or clients that these low prices are an everyday occurrence. It reminds them that they shouldn't expect similar specials anytime soon.

Because you often discounted prices at these events, on the surface, they may appear to be money losers. Many of the lead items at these events, will in fact loose money, but your goal is to get people in the front door, and you will accomplish that goal.

These events can be used as "turnaround" strategies for a low-volume business that has had difficulty due to bad management, low quality, poor customer services, or a substandard physical plant. Even when such serious problems have been corrected, it is often difficult to win customers back.

A Customer Appreciation Day is an event promotion that can prompt business during a slow time or draw customers back after a change of management. One version of this event was done by a Luby's in Tampa, Florida. This Luby's offered customers half-off everything for one day, a very strong offer indeed. To promote the event flyers were distributed door to door in a four-mile radius by the Luby's employees one week prior to the event. Posters were displayed both in the restaurant and in key places throughout the neighborhood. Table-tents were used inside the restaurant to inform regular customers about the promotion. Even though the goal of the promotion was to generate many new customers, the existing customers were instrumental in getting the word out. Ads were placed in the neighborhood newspapers several days before the event. The day of the event a large promotional balloon with the message "50 percent off" was flown above the building.

Luby's didn't have to spend much money on getting the word out in the week prior to the event. It didn't take a lot of advertising to make people aware of of such an attractive pricing offer.

A banjo player, a magician, and a balloon artist made the event festive and kept the large number of customers entertained while they waited to be seated. The interior of the restaurant was decorated to reinforce the festive spirit. Colorful balloons were everywhere.

Another key element was to make sure there was enough food to go around. This kind of promotion can be great for your business because you will get many new people to try your business. But if you upset them by not having enough product, than the event becomes a negative instead of a positive. The manager at Luby's knew from experience that with a promotion like this, the customers would tend to order the most expensive meals. So he stocked up on the items he knew would attract customer attention.

Not only do you need to have enough product on hand, you also need to make sure you have enough help. The manager at Luby's decided his promotion was so important that he asked all the other Luby's managers in the area to lend a helping hand. This proved to be a great help, because when the cafeteria was packed and the Luby's staff was under a great deal a pressure, they had experienced staff from other outlets to help them.

The result of the event was dramatic. Sales tripled for the day and customer counts quadrupled. More important, monthly sales went up 13 percent following the promotion. The manager guessed that at least half of the people coming to this event were new faces.

This is not the kind of promotion you can do on a regular basis. It's best used once or twice a year, usually during a slower period.

The Luby's promotion was very aggressive promotion, but look at it from a return-on-investment standpoint. Ask yourself how much money it would cost you to generate that kind of trial by new customers using traditional advertising media and a typical coupon offer. It could actually be much cheaper to offer your product at a ridiculously low price at a short-term event to pull in lots of new customers, than to spend a fortune on advertising.

Other examples of blow-out events include:

- A small restaurant chain rolled back its prices to those common in the 1950s. For one day only they offered hamburgers for 49¢, even though they regularly sold for $2.50.
- A gas station priced self-serve gas at 25¢ a gallon for one day, with a maximum of eight gallons per car per visit.
- A fast-food Mexican restaurant chain offered 29¢ tacos for one day at one location.
- A quick oil-change place offered $5 oil changes for one day at one location.
- A nightclub offered free beer and wine for one night.
- A pizza chain offered all the pizza you can eat for 99¢ for one day at one location.
- A frozen yogurt shop offered one free small yogurt for one day.
- A video rental franchise offered one free overnight video rental for one day at one location.

Other reason for blow-out promotions could include:

- A grand opening event
- A grand reopening event
- An anniversary event
- A remodeling event
- A new product introduction

Taking the Plunge

One college bookstore was able to get the jump on its competition by offering free bungie jumping with a textbook purchase. This turned what would normally be a simple sale into a major event. The cost was $5,000 for the bungie jumping equipment, but the promotion brought in over $75,000 in sales. The event drew new customers and generated big sales.

Outbound Blitz Marketing

Sometimes the event you hold isn't for your customers at your place of business. Instead it is for employees out in the community, who are drumming up business. This is an idea that is often used to get a new location up and running. This can be a day-long event or even a week-long event if you think that would be better.

First you need a group of people. The group will vary depending on your type of business. Some types will use their employees for this effort if there are enough employees. Other types of businesses will borrow managers from other stores in their chain or franchise from nearby areas.

The goal is simple The group canvases the neighborhood to distribute fliers, coupons, free cards, door hangers, or whatever you decide you need to get people in the front door. Chick-fil-A, a successful fast food chicken chain, uses free sandwich cards. This company is more than willing to give away that first sandwich because it knows that a customer tries its good food, he or she will probably come back.

A bank got its neighboring branch managers together for a day to canvass a neighborhood. Since branch managers are not trained to comfortable in a cold-calling situation, they visit the area businesses in groups of three, giving them safety in numbers. They introduce themselves, and then hand out cards, literature, and a premium gift like a glass jar filled with candy. Then they ask a few questions about the business's banking needs. Strong leads are followed up later by that branch manager.

To make these marketing-blitz efforts successful, follow these guidelines:

1. Assign territory for each participant so you don't overlap. For sales-reluctant people, assign small groups.
2. Everybody goes out at the same time. If you split up, meet someplace for lunch and review your progress and fire each other up again.
3. Have specific printed pieces to distribute. Anything like a free trial will be more effective. Give out plenty of business cards and give people a reason to visit your business. Every person who runs or manages a business should have business cards.
4. In selling services, ask a few questions to uncover needs and potential future business.
5. Limit the time out. A day or two is best, and never spend longer than a week. If you stretch out too long you'll begin to waste time. The tighter the timetable, the higher the energy.
6. Don't spend too much time with any one customer. If need be, make an appointment for a later time.

Chapter Summary

Blow-out promotions are usually single-day, single-location events where prices have been dropped so low that customers will stand in line for hours to visit your business. They can be done once or twice a year.

Customer appreciation events are celebrations with activities and attractions to create a party atmosphere, as well as aggressive pricing.

Blitzing a neighborhood is an inexpensive way to meet neighbors and distribute promotional material like business cards, discount cards, free cards, flyers, door hangers, and so on.

7

On-Site Marketing

Promoting within your own store or office is usually the least expensive, least time-consuming, and most effective marketing you can do. Whenever people come in to shop or they are waiting to be served, you have an opportunity for communication that could lead to additional sales. In this chapter you'll read about Streetfighter Marketing techniques that you totally control. Unlike a cross-promotion, a value card, or a community-involvement program, these ideas require no cooperation from other businesses or groups in the community to facilitate distribution.

I know an orthodontist who put a Space Invaders video arcade game in his reception area in the mid-1970s, when that game was the hottest thing around. Later he added a Pac Man game. Kids could play for free while they waited to see the dentist. These same kids would go back to school after an appointment and tell the other kids about the free video games in their orthodonist's office. Those kids would then ask their parents to take them to that particular orthodontist when they needed their teeth straightened. I'm sure in a few years he'll be the first dental office to offer virtual-reality games to this patients.

In a store, you can get creative with your signs, "point of purchase" (POP) displays, or "point of sale" (POS) displays. Video-rental stores are picking up on this reality and using simple small signs attached to the shelves called "shelf-talkers" for cross-selling. They inform the renter that if he or she liked a certain movie that other, perhaps lesser known, titles with a similar plot or the same actors, or the same directors are available. For example, the notice may suggest to the renter that "If you liked *Hunt for Red October* you might want to consider *Patriot Games, Das Boat,* or *Ice Station Zebra.*"

Grocery stores, convenience stores, and drug stores benefit from the same approach by suggesting their more profitable private-label brand instead of the nationally recognized brand-name products. When the customer is buying turkey for Thanksgiving, the shelf talker reminds him about the stuffing, cranberry sauce, yams, and pumpkin pie he should also buy, listing by aisle where each of the items can be found. Since each of those other items also have shelf talkers, no matter which item the customer picks first, he will find signs recommending the other four items.

Selling by suggestion is a great use of internal displays. The full-service car wash that wants to promote use of such options as wax, Amorall, and scent has a better chance of selling those items by making customers aware of them. Restaurants often push deserts, appetizers, and cocktails with table tents, placemats, and other displays. When I was having my car's oil changed at a tire dealer's shop near my office, I noticed a sign for a package of five oil changes for $59. Thus the package price was a bit less than $12 per oil change. Even with a coupon the cheapest I've been able to get one for is about $16, so the package offered a real savings. If I hadn't noticed the sign I would have had no reason to return to this tire dealers shop. But because of that sign the dealer had an opportunity to make a bigger sale and to keep me as a loyal customer for the better part of a year.

The clever manager of a Super Valu grocery store noted an influx of Russian emigrants into the neighborhood and got a jump on his two competitors by hiring some of the Russian students to translate the Super Valu's sales messages into Russian. Thus he captured almost all of that segment of the market. An equally clever Diary Queen franchisee had all his employees wear buttons that said "See you tomorrow" and also ordered them to repeat that same message to their customers when they left with their purchases. He noticed an increase in customer frequency thanks to these simple ideas.

Hair stylists are notorious for *not* suggesting hair-care products to their customers. A salon owner I know dealt with this problem by putting a bottle of shampoo at each station with a sign that said, "Ask your stylist about this great shampoo." Once the customer asked, the stylist had to respond and sales of that product increased.

Internal signs in general help sales. Even if you don't have a special sale or discount program, you can use internal signs to inform your customers of the features and benefits of particular products and services.

Printing with a Secondary Purpose

Streetfighter Marketers always look for *free* ways to communicate with their customers. There are many such opportunities right in your own office or store. Think, for example, of the family restaurants that use paper placemats or the fast-food places that use tray liners to market various menu items. Restaurants have to use placemats of some sort, so instead of buying preprinted generic ones, print up your own to use as promotional tools.

Whether you have one restaurant or a chain of five hundred, get your printer to make placemats with a colored logo and borders. Leave the middle at the mats blank so they can be "overprinted" by the local quick printer with seasonal or promotional messages. If your restaurant is sponsoring a community-service event, promote it on the placemats for one week. This is a very effective form of advertising. Combine placemat advertising with posters, table tents, window banners, register cards, and possibly a movable-type sign outside your restaurant, and you can give a neighborhood promotion a big boost at minimal cost.

Remember, however, that you don't want to make your store or office look trashy. You can reach the point of "overkill" that could offend your customers. I bank at the Bank One branch in Gahanna. This parent bank does a great job of creating banners, counter cards, envelope stuffers, and so on, to advertise its services, and the branch bank does a tasteful job of displaying them. The displays are effective without overkill and never look trashy.

There are any number of other printed items that you could use to carry a message for your business. Think about using invoices, checks, envelopes, and estimate sheets. Auto-repair stores that use paper floor mats to protect the car carpeting could use them to carry a message. When I owned a nightclub years ago I developed a paper coaster to replace cocktail napkins. The pieces were printed on card stock, were 4 1/4" square, and were printed four to a sheet of paper at our local quick printer. I used a standard logo and border for every batch printed and could customize my message according to my needs. Every time the bartender slapped down a coaster on the table before setting down the drink, the advertising message made it's impression. Most postage meters can be rigged to include a message. For about $50 you can have a special "slug" created that will print a slogan or other short message next to your metered postage.

Computer Banners and Signs

There are very inexpensive computer programs that can help you make banners and signs for your store or office. According to the computer retailers, the most popular one is called "Print Shop Deluxe." This is one of the most cost-effective ways of making internal signs and produces a quality product that is much better than most hand-drawn signs. If you need a banner in a hurry, this can be a great way to go.

Quick Signs Done Professionally

If you're more concerned about appearance, you may want to have your banners and signs, especially those that will carry messages you plan to use for a while, done professionally. There are a growing number of professional sign companies that specialize in quick turnaround at a reasonable price. Some of these franchised sign companies include Fast Signs, Mr. Sign, Signs Now!, Speedy Sign-A-Rama, Signs by Tomorrow, and Sign Express. Some franchises offer more service than others, but you'll find they all can handle a variety of needs from temporary signs to more permanent signs.

Leveraging Your Internal Signs

Not only is using signs to communicate with your customers valuable for your business, it may be just as valuable to other area businesses. You might be able to leverage another business's exposure to your customers into a "promotional currency" of sorts and turn that into a means to bring in new customers.

Unfortunately, most merchants who routinely put printed material in front of their customers don't realize the true value of this kind of exposure to other area merchants. They often sell the exposure on their register tapes, placemats, or other internal printed pieces for peanuts. Independent grocery store operators, for example, reach almost 97 percent of the households in their neighborhood on a regular basis. Exposure such as this could be invaluable to many other area business. Why give register-tape exposure away for free or just a small compensation when you can turn it into a promotional powerhouse? With the Streetfighter Marketing approach you can turn this minuscule money generator into a massive promotional tool.

Instead of collecting a few pennies to display someone else's advertising, why not demand a cross-promotion in which another area business is required to really promote your business in exchange for exposure on your register tapes, placemats, or whatever. This has the most impact when your business is one that has a major customer count a grocery store, a convenience store, a high-volume gas station, a drug store, a department store, or a fast-food restaurant. Then you're in the drivers seat. You can demand that your cross-promotion partner do certificate distribution, mailers, signs, and displays, and or even that it mention you in its newspaper, TV, radio, or outdoor advertising. This kind of exposure will be worth a great deal more to you than the free register-tape or placemat exposure you offer in return to your partner.

When I owned my nightclub I got a lot of free advertising exposure. Other businesses would mention the club in their advertising if I let them have a portion of one week's worth of coasters to display their own messages. In one case a stereo store gave me a $600 car audio system to give away as the grand prize in a contest in exchange for exposure on my coasters. Radio stations increased my club's ad schedule significantly at no cost to me for similar exposure. I had created my own internal advertising medium. Then, instead of trying to sell space on this medium and getting very little for it, I used it in the form of barter for to obtain what I wanted for my business.

Publicity Reprint and Postings

When you get good local press coverage, you can extend its impact by having the article reprinted. Most local publications are more than willing to give you permission to reprint a review of your restaurant, for example, or an article that gives your shop or service favorable mention, so long as the reprint includes the publication's name. You can copy the article directly if it's short, or have it reduced if it's lengthy so it will fit on a single sheet. Then insert it in your billing, mailings, newsletters, or other correspondence with your customers. You can also have the article enlarged by your quick printer and then mounted on foamboard. An enlarged poster-size article makes a great display in your store or office. Another approach, especially for an office instead of a retail store, is to have an original copy of the article professionally framed or mounted and embossed on a wood plaque with an engraved metal plate at the bottom commemorating the item. Obviously, this approach is more expensive than creating a foam board poster, but the tasteful display that results is perfect for the office of a doctor, lawyer, or other professional. Depending on the size of the article, this option could run you between $75 and $150 at your local frame shop or trophy company.

Parking-Lot Attention Getters

To draw attention to your location you could do something unusual in the parking lot. For example, the Parker Shelton School of Karate had a location on a busy street in Fort Wayne, Indiana. The landlord would not give the school's owner permission to put up a sign near the street so the only sign he had to identify his school was on the building itself. The sign was small and so far from the street that passing motorists couldn't see it. So, during the summer, the instructors often took their karate classes outside to the parking lot near the street. Imagine the sight of forty karate students in their white gis (uniforms) all kicking, punching, and yelling in unison. This unusual parking-lot display caught the eyes of thousands of motorists—many of whom were potential customers—over the course of the summer.

You may have a supplier who can provide you with banners or

special inflatable signs. One well-known luggage manufacturer has a four-story inflatable gorilla that it rents to its dealers for a reasonable fee. It turns a lot of heads. Many breweries and soft-drink manufacturers can provide their dealers with large inflatable versions of their canned and bottled products. One steak-house chain has a huge inflatable steer that can be trailored to any location for promotions.

Another way to draw attention is to hire actors or to dress employees in costume. You might use Santa Claus or the Easter Bunny, a superhero, or a mascot somehow related to your business logo. Mascots are particularly useful. Someone dressed as your company mascot can be used in your public relations efforts: the mascot can pay regular visits to the children's hospital, make appearances at local malls, and even get on TV.

Tom Bramlett of Scuba Unlimited in Pleasanton, California, was faced with a new competitor opening up near one of his stores. The new competitor spent a small fortune on radio advertising. To help customers locate his new store, the competitor used the tag line, "Just look for the big blue balloon." Being the Streetfighter that he is, Tom Bramlett quickly bought his own blue balloon, one that happened to be bigger and bluer than the new competitor's. Many people seeking the new store ended up at Bramlett's store instead; the blue-balloon ploy generated a great deal of sales at little cost to Bramlett, while simultaneously deflating his competitor.

Giant balloons and minature blimps are a powerful on-site way to draw attention to your location. Many businesses pay a premium for a high-traffic location but they often need something extra to really leverage that location. According to Scott Zimmer, president of Giant Advertising in Costa Mesa, California, "Retailers can see an increase in foot traffic as much as tenfold and an increase in sales of 30 percent to over 100 percent is not unusual by using inflatable advertising two hundred feet in the air."[2]

Frequency Cards

Another aspect of on-site marketing is determining what you can do to encourage a customer to come back to buy from you repeatedly. Many businesses use frequent-purchase programs.

VIP cards are issued to customers by just about every major airline and hotel chain as part of their frequent user programs. The only problem with these programs is that, since *every* airline and hotel chain has one, none of these businesses comes out ahead. It seems to me that the companies that offer VIP cards don't get that much of an advantage, but if one didn't offer VIP cards it would be at a great disadvantage.

When starting a VIP card program you want to make sure that you are influencing customers to behave the way you want them to, and not just giving away dollars. Also, consider what would happen if you were to stop the program. How would it impact your sales? How would your customers react? Every so often one of the airlines changes its rules to make it a little more difficult to redeem a free ticket. That's an annoying practice that cuts into the customer loyalty that airline tried to build in the first place.

One very important point: whenever your customer uses his or her freebie, discount, reward, or whatever, treat him or her just like a cash-paying customer. When I use my free airline tickets, I notice that I'm not treated the same as when I use a purchased ticket. Now I'm a second-class citizen. Ticket agents are quick to point out that because the ticket was-free, "I should be happy with what they give me. But I'm quick to respond, Do you know how many full-fare flights I've paid for to get this "free" ticket?" They forget that those who use frequent-flier redemptions should be treated to the best care because they are the airlines best customers.

When you provide your customers with a VIP card, you had better resolve to treat those customers like VIPs or the VIP card means nothing. Customers will recognize that you're trying to pull a fast one on them and your policy will backfire on you. Whether it's a special price, access, treatment, terms, attention, or whatever, live up to your promise.

The Prepaid VIP Card

Another way to use a VIP-card approach is with a prepaid service, product, or membership. Providing a prepay discount program is a great way to shore up your customer base. Once these customers prepay for something, they're less likely to go elsewhere for the duration of the discount program.

One video store chain offers a prepay VIP card for which you pay a certain amount up-front, but which saves you a considerable amount when you rent your movies. The prepay system is great for improving cash flow during a slow time. Moreover, it also stimulates customers to come into your store more often: having prepaid to buy the card, they don't' want it to go to waste.

Restaurants have VIP membership programs too. You pay a certain amount up-front and thereafter receive a discount on meals. One common practice is to offer one meal at full price and one meal at half price whenever the VIP cardholder dines with a companion. Restaurant owners are pleased with the results they get from offering VIP cards. The cardholders dine out more frequently, and they often buy more expensive meals.

Many comic-book stores have a VIP service. Often their best customers will buy the same three or four titles each week. The comic-book store owner makes an arrangement with these customers to pull those titles for them and often gives them a discount too. One problem with this service is that comic buyers aren't very prompt about coming in to pick up their "set-aside" comic books. This system doesn't make sense to me. Why offer a discount when you're providing an additional service?

By turning this service into a prepay service, however, you would have a legitimate reason to offer a discount. The comic-book store owner might offer a three-month, a six-month, and a twelve-month "subscription service." The longer the term for the service, the deeper the discount. If they paid for their VIP service up-front, the customers would show up promptly; moreover the owner would have a commitment from them to be his customer for that term.

Punch Cards

Another card kind that retailers frequently use is called the "punch card"; each time you make a purchase, the retailer punches your card, and when the card is full of punches you receive a free item. Punch cards are given to existing customers to keep them loyal or to motivate them to increase their number of purchases. Punch cards can be an effective marketing tool. The strategy I like to use with these cards is to time the promotion to give me a little boost during an anticipated slow time.

Let's say you know that business always fall off in your store right after the first of the year. Your average customer buys from you weekly. You plan a frequency-promotion offer based on the slogan "Buy five and get the sixth one free." Distribute the punch cards to your customers around the beginning of December. By the end of the year most of your regular weekly participants will have made four or five purchases and will be just one or two purchases away from receiving a free item. So they'll return to your store during your slow time in the first couple weeks of January to make the one or two more purchases they need to earn their freebie. Thus the punch cards help to create business in a slower time.

One very interesting frequency promotion was developed by Pam Bly of All Kitchens, a buyers group for some 120 wholesale food distributors throughout the country. All Kitchen's customers typically sell food wholesale to restaurants and institutions. To help their distributors, All Kitchens provided them with a program called "Junior Sports Club." The goal was to provide family restaurants with a special menu and incentives to attract children from ages seven to fifteen. All Kitchens's research had revealed that this age group greatly influenced parents' decisions about which family restaurant to patronize. Yet, no one really catered to this age group.

All Kitchens's distributors supplied restaurants with frequency punch cards (see Figure 7–1). When a child in the target age group dined at a participating restaurant he or she would be enrolled in the club and get a card. Every time the child returned (with his or her family) the card was punched. After a certain number of punches the children earned free gifts. A special menu was created to further attract these kids, one that featured real food rather than "cutesy" kid food. The portions were smaller than those on the adult menu and priced accordingly. The children enjoyed being treated as young adults, rather than "Kiddies."

For children's gifts, the restaurant operator could buy premiums like T-shirts, fanny packs, sippie cups, and so on. If they are real Streetfighters, they can do some horse trading with area merchants like the music store, bookstore, bike shop, athletic shoe store, electronics store, and so on. The operator collects sample prizes to display at the restaurant, and instead of giving these prizes directly to the children, gives them special certificates they take to the merchant for redemption. Participating merchants like this system because it brings customers into their stores.

FIGURE 7–1
A frequency card can motivate repeat business.

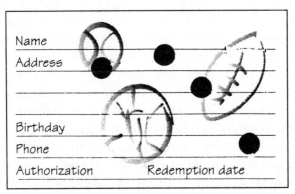

Name

Address

Birthday

Phone

Authorization   Redemption date

This is a good example of how neighborhood marketing is working its way up the distribution chain. One of the All Kitchen's distributors who is very successful at this kind of marketing is J. King Distribution in Long Island, New York. The owner, John King, focuses on his customer's needs while his competition concentrates on price. King works with his suppliers like General Mills, Tropicana, and so on, to provide his customers as much marketing support as possible. He even has a couple of people on staff whose responsibility it is to help develop local promotions and provide the collateral material to go with it—at no charge to his customers.

He has created a value-added relationship with his customers. When they need help, either he provides it himself or finds someone who can. Many manufacturers will make products, marketing materials, and even money available to help local businesses better promote their products. Often it's a complicated process to take advantage of these special opportunities. King makes sure his manufacturers keep him informed about every new opportunity, and then he handles the logistics of matching these manufacturer programs with his customers that want them.

With someone like King taking the initiative, each level of participation benefits: manufacturer, distributor, and retailer. King is able to use these opportunities to solidify relationships with his customers, thereby making it more difficult for a competitor to get a foothold by simply knocking a few pennies of the price.

Coupon Booklets

A variation on the VIP card is the coupon booklet. A third party gathers offers from a number of businesses, puts them all together in a coupon booklet, and then sells the booklet to students or some other target group. The most widely known of these is the Entertainment Book. A typical coupon book might include a number of two-meals-for-the-price-of-one offers from area restaurants, discount passes to movie theaters, free items or dollars-off deals at music stores, bookstores, and other merchants, and free or discount services such as dry cleaning, bike rentals, manicures, and the like. From a consumer point of view, such coupon books are a great deal if you can take advantage of enough of the offers. From a business perspective, these books can be a good way to introduce yourself to some new customers.

As long as you put some restrictions on usage (for example, restaurants might want coupons to be redeemed on slow weekday nights) so you're not turning away full-paying customers to honor these offers, you really have little to loose. Make sure your staff treat those customers who come in to redeem coupons like VIPs. The purpose of participating in this kind of program is to induce some new people to give your store a try. If you treat them poorly because they're getting a two-for-one deal or a big discount on something you sell, they'll hold it against you and never come back.

It's always a good idea to get new customers on your mailing list so you can send them something to entice them to return again. You may have to offer a little value the second time out, but it will be worth it if the new customer becomes a regular customer.

Though these certificate programs usually involve deep discounts, your price credibility is protected since the user had to buy by the coupon book to get the offer. Think carefully before joining if you have to pay any kind of fee to be included in the coupon-book program. The program may not be cost-effective if you offer a costly coupon and also pay for right to do so. If you're paying to participate, even if only for a "set-up" charge, put reasonable limits on the offers and when they can be redeemed.

FIGURE 7–2
Turn your customers into Streetfighters for you.

```
GUEST PASS
Parker Shelton Judo & Karate

GUEST MEMBER_____
        IS ENTITLED TO 50% OFF THE REGULAR PRICE OF THE
            INTRODUCTORY LESSONS. YOU SAVE $9.75.
                     INCLUDES:
        • SELF DEFENSE        • SUN TAN BOOTH
        • SAUNA & STEAM BOOTH • WEIGHT TRAINING
        • BODY CONDITIONING   • COMPETITION

GUEST OF_____ RANK_____ "Be The Best"
        If under 18 years of age must be accompanied by parent.
```

Customer-Incentive Programs

You may not have thought of customers as marketing allies, but you should do so. Customer referrals are the lifeblood of any business. They are the least expensive and most effective way to get more customers. If you do a good job, you'll get some customer referrals naturally. But there are ways to encourage your happy customers to send more customers your way. Instead of just hoping that new cus-

FIGURE 7–3
Both the existing customers and the new ones get rewarded.

```
SAVE A FRIEND 10%
at 20TH CENTURY AUTOMOTIVE
1001 LEESBURG ROAD • FORT WAYNE, INDIANA

MY FRIEND_____
        WOULD LIKE TO SAVE 10% ON THIS AUTOMOTIVE REPAIR.
        APPLIES TO LABOR ONLY. PARTS NOT INCLUDED.
        CANNOT BE COMBINED WITH ANY OTHER DISCOUNT
                     OR SPECIAL OFFER
RECOMMENDED BY_____ DATE___/___/___
        CALL FOR AN APPOINTMENT 432-5325

"IF WE CAN'T FIX IT, IT CAN'T BE FIXED!"
```

tomers come your way, you can encourage them to do so if you have a customer-referral program in place.

Customers get excited after making expensive purchases, such as exercise equipment, real estate, interior decorating, or appliances. When they are in this excited state, they are most likely to refer business. One way to exploit this excited state is to create some customer referral cards that your newly satisfied customer can hand out to friends. The card should allow for some special value (a discount, a value-added, a free-gift, or the like) when redeemed. Have your customer sign the card so that if his or her friend comes into your store to shop, you can reward the initial customer him or her with a discount on future purchase, a free gift, or even cash. Give the new customer three to five cards, and promise more if they want them. (See Figures 7–2 and 7–3 for examples of successful customer cards.)

Remembering the Customer

A good memory is one of the least expensive promotional tools you could have in your business. Imagine if you went to a restaurant and were greeted by name by the host or server. You would want to go back: not because of low prices, not necessarily because of the quality of the food, not because it's convenient, but because you felt special when you were recognized and addressed by name.

In a business where your good customers have contact with you on a weekly basis, this type of customer service could be worth $100,000 in advertising, yet it costs you practically nothing. This applies to restaurants, dry cleaners, video rental, car washes, drugstores, grocery stores, convenience stores, gas stations, anyplace where you see your customers on a regular basis. There are a number of courses, books, and cassettes available to help you learn how to remember names and faces.[3]

Meet The Manager

One of the easiest sales builders to initiate is to have the manager or owner of the business personally hand out twenty business cards each week out in the community. When a potential customer meets the owner or manager it makes that potential customer feel special and increases the liklihood that they will be buy from their new acaintance's business. You have the option of offering a special sav-

FIGURE 7–4

One location got 14,000 certificates out with 2,547 redeemed. Guest counts were up 13.2 percent for the month.

ings or added value by writing it on the back of the business card. It's not uncommon to see a 25 to 50 percent return on this type of personized distribution.

Employee-Incentive Contests

Your employees can be another effective on-site marketing tool. A surefire way to get your employees hustling to bring you new business is a contest I call the Streetfighter's Employee Incentive Contest. Each employee, full- and part-time, receives a number of special-value cards. I usually begin with fifty. The card entitles the bearer to a savings or value-added at your business. This offer should be just a little better than offers you may use for cross-promotions. Be sure to include an expiration date on the card; I suggest thirty days from when you expect the last of the cards to be distributed. (Sample special-value cards for employees are illustrated in Figures 7–4, 7–5, and 7–6.)

Each card should have a signature line for the employees to sign to make the card valid. Giving your employees the power to validate the value-added cards will make them feel special, and it will enable you to track whose cards are begin redeemed. Your employee will feel he or she is an important component in the success of your business. By having the employee sign each card, you are actually transferring the responsibility of offering the savings from you

FIGURE 7–5
Get employees to hand out your advertising for you on their own time.

**BRING A FRIEND TO PIZZA HUT®
FOR LUNCH,
AND WE'LL FEED YOUR FRIEND
FOR HALF PRICE!**

Buy one of our delicious Lunch Combinations at the regular menu price, and your friend can buy one of equal value for HALF-PRICE! 11 am to 3 pm, M-F.

VALID ONLY THROUGH MARCH 31, 1982 AND ONLY AT:

**The East State Pizza Hut®
restaurant**
3820 East State at The Bypass
Fort Wayne, Indiana Phone 483-9531

Authorized By _____

to the employee. The employee and the person who receives the card will think that this savings is made possible by knowing somebody on the "inside."

Once the value cards have been printed and handed out to all employees, the contest begins. The employees' goal is to distribute these cards to family, friends, and acquaintances in their neighborhood.

Rules

Participation in the contest should be optional. I've found that this promotion works best when I actually ask for volunteers to participate in the contest. Later, if others want to join in, it's no problem. Employees have the chance to win prizes, but there are a few rules they must follow if they choose to participate. What are the rules? First, the cards cannot be passed out to existing customers. Second, distribution must be done on the employees' own time. Third, distribution must take place beyond the parking lot of the business: absolutely no handing out cards at the business location. Occasionally you will find an employee who will break one of these rules.

FIGURE 7–6
Sometimes teams of employees work harder.

You can deal with each situation in your own way. The contest should last no longer than one month. After a while your employees will get tired of the contest. Also, the cards should be passed out in the first week of the contest.

Checking Results

There are two ways you can check the results of the contest. One way is to count the total number of cards redeemed. Whichever employee has the most cards redeemed is the winner; the second-most number of cards, second place; and so on. Another method of checking results is to add up the total amount of the gross sales. When the card is redeemed, the sales slip is stapled to it. At the end of the contest, the sale slips are added up, and the employee with the highest sales is the winner.

If you use the latter method, you will encourage your employees to hand out their value cards to individuals whom they judge capable of spending more money with your business. For example, they might give the value card to a parent of a large family who is more likely to buy for the entire family than to someone who will only be buying for himself.

Remember: this contest gets all your employees involved in the promotion, from clerical workers, to bookkeepers, to dishwashers, to janitors. Not only are you getting the cards distributed free, but you are subtly getting one of the best forms of advertising, organized word-of-mouth advertising.

Prizes

The prizes are essential to make this contest fun and profitable for employees. I suggest that the majority of the prizes be traded out with other businesses. Examples could be car washes, CDs or cassettes, movie passes, gift certificates for dinners, clothing certificates, and so on. Find out what kinds of prizes your employees want. For a grand prize, you may want to offer a stereo or a color TV. One of the most effective grand prizes I've used is a day off with pay. Even though in most cases the cost of a day off with pay is much less than other possible grand prizes, it seems to get a great response.

It is very important that everyone wins something. If an employee participates in the contest, and has at least one card redeemed, then that employee should get something for his or her efforts. You could also have weekly winners, with a grand-prize winner at the end of the contest.

Another element that can add to the contest's success is to divide the volunteers into teams of three or four. In addition to the individual prizes for the first-, second-, and third-place winners, you could also offer a team prize like a pizza or ice cream party.

The Suggested-Sell Contest

This is a contest for those employees who actually take care of the customers. A hardware store ran a suggested-sell contest for one week. Each person out on the floor was given a number of certificates good for a special price on lightbulbs. Unlike the certificates distributed in the employee-incentive contest I described earlier, these certificates were distributed to customers *in the store*. The employees asked each customers if he or she needed lightbulbs. Just about everyone did. The employee signed his or her name to the certificate before giving it to the customer and the results were tracked. The three employees with the most redemptions won prizes.

Selling-through-suggestion contests are a great way to get your salesclerks to recommend that one extra item. It's a lot easier to add 10 percent to an existing sale than to get a whole new sale.

Floor Sales

Training your floor salespeople is critical to business success. Most showroom salespeople are awful. They may have great product knowledge but their sales skills are very weak. Harry Friedman, author of *Successful Retail Selling*, has sound advice about how to improve your salespeople's sales skills.[4]

One of Freidman's techniques that I really like is what he calls the "180 degree turn around approach." For most retail sales, the clerk will approach the customer directly and ask something like, "May I help you?" The customer then usually responds, "No thanks, I'm just looking." That response is the kiss of death in retail selling. So you want to adapt a technique so that the customer doesn't immediately put up a wall to protect himself or herself from the pesky salesperson.

Freidman's approach is to walk by the customer, looking in the other direction as if he were looking for something. He takes about four or five steps past the customer, then acts as if he suddenly realizes that there is a customer there. He turns around 180 degrees, and then speaks. This walk-by approach helps to reduce the customer's anxiety.

Freidman also hates openers like "May I help you?" because they automatically invite a negative response. He suggests opening with something conversational instead of a question. He calls this "schmoozing" and claims that it is another technique to reduce customer anxiety.

Chapter Summary

There are numerous Streetfighting opportunities that you can initiate at your business without having to seek the cooperation of other area businesses.

Drawing additional attention to your business location can be done with inexpensive signs and banners. Having demonstrations, tents, sales, costumed characters, or inflatable signs in the parking lot can draw attention to your business from the passing traffic.

Taking care of the customer once they've walked through the front door is critical to repeat business. Remembering the names of regular customers can be a big incentive for customers to buy from you.

Contests for employees and customers motivate them to bring in their friends and relatives to the business. Suggested-selling contests help increase the amount of each sale by motivating those employees who have contact with customers to recommend one more item.

8

Mail Pitches that Don't Get Pitched

Direct mail is one of the few forms of traditional advertising that allows you target a very specific audience, both geographically and demographically. There are countless uses for direct-mail advertising, such that billions of dollars are spent on it every year. The vast majority of direct mail, especially bulk mailings, is considered "junk" and gets immediately trashed. The Streetfighter Marketing approach to direct mail increases the readership and impact of your direct mailings so that your return on investment is much higher.

Postcard Profits

One of the biggest problems with most direct-mail campaigns is simply to get your advertising message read. Most "junk mail" is tossed in the trash even before the envelope is opened. So creating mail pieces that at least invite the recipients to look at them puts you way ahead of the pack.

One way to get people to see your advertising message is to put it on the back of a picture postcard of a vacation spot. Picture postcards of vacation spots get attention because they don't look like advertising. A person receiving a picture postcard from Disneyworld, for example, is going to be curious about who they know that went to Disneyworld. They'll turn it over and read it.

121

Wish You Were Here

Picture postcards can have a tremendous impact when the picture is of an exotic vacation spot that in some way relates to your business. For example, the owner of a scuba-diving business in California generated a mailing list of customers who had expressed interest in one of her package dive trips but had yet to go on one. Through contacts at Cancan, Cozemel, Hawaii, and the Caymen Islands, she bought a number of picture postcards prior to her trips. While still at home, she addressed the cards and wrote a message reminding the potential customer of the next diving opportunity. Half-way through the trip the postcards were mailed. This approach would also work for travel agencies, cruise lines, and vacation packagers. The mailing list would consist of the names of anyone who has inquired about trips or the names of past customers who might be considering another vacation sometime in the future.

I'm Here for You

Another version of the picture-postcard approach is useful for those businesses whose owners travel to exotic places for the benefit of the customers or clients. Training and buying trips are two examples. A jewelry store owner from Iowa who goes to New York, Antwerp, and Tel Aviv on a diamond-buying trip would make a great impact on her customers if she sent them postcards from those cities with a message about giving them the best quality at the lowest price by eliminating the middleman. The same technique would work for a clothing retailer who visits Singapore, Hong Kong, and Taiwan, where the clothes are being manufactured. The postcard in this case could suggest that the manager or owner is ensuring quality work.

The same applies when you travel to a seminar or conference where you're getting cutting-edge information to benefit your clients, customers, or patients. Mailing a picture postcard from Washington, D.C., to your legal clients in St. Louis to let them know that you're getting valuable insights into the impact of the latest tax changes, or Supreme Court decision, or environmental law would impress most of them.

FIGURE 8–1
A postcard mailer that helps get calls returned.

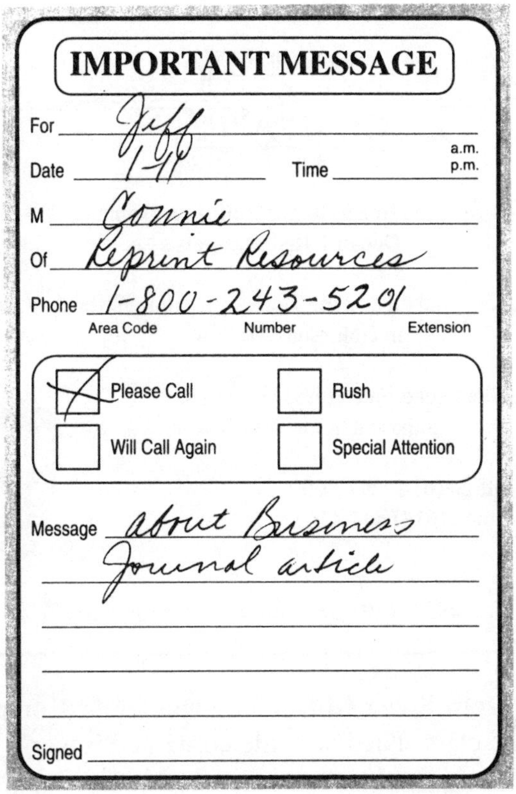

IMPORTANT MESSAGE

For Jeff

Date 1-11 Time a.m. p.m.

M Connie

Of Reprint Resources

Phone 1-800-243-5201
Area Code Number Extension

- [x] Please Call
- [ ] Rush
- [ ] Will Call Again
- [ ] Special Attention

Message about Business Journal article

Signed

While You Were Out

One postcard that really gets attention is used by the sales reps at Reprint Resources in Kansas City, Missouri (see Figure 8–1). It is a 4” x 6” pink card that is printed to resemble a telephone message slip. The rep handwrites a message asking the customer to call her. The card looks like it came from the customer’s own office. The front side has Reprint Resource’s address, its slogan, the mailing label, and the postage-meter imprint for 19¢.

Junk Mail?

One of the more clever direct-mail campaigns was used by a realtor (see Figure 8–2). The first mailer was a simple 5 1/2 x 4 1/4 one-

FIGURE 8–2

This two-step mailer got lots of attention.

**Success in Buying or Selling a Home
Doesn't Just Happen**

Count on Roger Mitchell and the Team of Realtors® for Best Results
in Columbus Midtown

* Buyers & Sellers get a Free Home Warranty
  when you list or purchase a home with Roger

Office (614) 297-8600
Home (614) 444-4103

* Valid 2/93 thru 5/93   1 per transaction at closing

color postcard from Roger Mitchell of Dooley & Company Realtors mailed third class. The back side contained Roger's photo and an offer to provide a free home warranty with a listing or purchase. The postcard was nothing spectacular and most recipients must have trashed it after glancing at it.

A week later Mitchell mailed a second mailing in standard business envelopes same homes via first-class postage. Inside the envelopes was the same postcard he had sent earlier, but now looking like it had been crumpled up and then flattened. Attached to the "decrumpled" postcard was a handwritten note that read, "Please don't throw this away again! Roger Mitchell. Thanks!" The first reaction of recipients of this mailing was "How did this guy get this back? Did he go through our trash?" In reality it was a planned second mailing. It got a lot of local attention, including a free article in the neighborhood newspaper. The third mailing was a letter. Instead of getting trashed, it got read.

Database Postcards

Nonpicture postcards can also be useful. Very plain postcards are used successfully for reminders concerning appointments and commitments. I receive postcards from my dentist, my car dealership's service department, my kid's shoe store, and my florist (around my wife's, mother's, and mother-in-law's birthday and my anniversary).

Though you could use any piece of mail and not necessarily a postcard, I think a postcard mailing used in conjunction with a well-defined customer database can be one of the most important marketing tools you have at your disposal. The more you know about your customers' needs, the more sales you can make with this approach. Consider a fine men's clothing store. When I buy my first suit there, the salesperson should record some important information about me. He will obviously have my name and home phone but he should also ask for my business phone and address. He should know my wife's name and her business phone number and address. He should know my birthday and my anniversary. He knows my suit size, but he should inquire about my tastes, for example, in suits and better casual ware. With this information he can market very effectively and inexpensively when the opportunity arises.

Suppose the store just received a new shipment of Georgio Armani suits. A simple postcard or even a phone call to me at my office might well prompt me to come in and take a look at the suits. This practice costs practically nothing, and because they are targeting my specific needs I will pay attention.

Suppose a couple of weeks before my birthday they send a postcard or make a call to my wife. They know my birthday is just around the corner and they just happen to have some great slacks and sweaters in my size that they know I've been interested in. They suggest she come in to take a look or, if she wants, because our credit card number is on file, they can ship out the slacks and a sweater today. If she doesn't like them, she can bring them back and they'll find something perfect. That's service. It takes some organization and effort but when businesses do this kind of thing for customers, they hold on to those customers.

Less Postage, Works Great

One other big advantage of postcard mailers, provided the postcard you use is not oversized, is that you can mail it at the postcard rate. At this time that is 10¢ less than the regular first-class rate yet a postcard gets handled as if it were first-class mail.

Invitation to New Sales

Another type of mail piece that gets high readership is the invitation mailer. When you get a wedding invitation in the mail, for example, you immediately open it. Getting your mail piece opened and looked at is half the battle, so if you make your mail piece look just like a wedding invitation your readership goes up dramatically. Like with the picture-postcard approach, you tie the headline of your offer to the invitation theme: "We Invite You to Save Money" or "You're Cordially Invited to Our Sales Event."

To make full impact in your invitation mailer, use the following guidelines.

1.   It is expensive to use an actual wedding invitation but you can achieve the same effect by printing your piece on textured paper, with a vertical format, 5 1/2 x 8 1/2 folded over to 5 1/2 x 4 1/4. That size is printed two to a sheet of paper (two-up), so to print one thousand you only need five hundred sheets. Your quick printer will have matching envelopes. If you use a larger size, it will cost you more because that's a custom design. *Use an italic typestyle that resembles a wedding invitation but not one that is so fancy or ornate that it's difficult to read.* You can use raised print if you like, but offset printing is usually less expensive, is printed on premises, and should work fine.

Every once in a while your quick printer or stationary store might have actual invitations that have been discontinued or dramatically reduced in price. It's a long shot but worth checking out. Compare the cost of using real invitations with the cost of creating your own "mock" invitations. If the real ones are not too much more expensive and their style is impressive you may want to go ahead and use them.

2.   Print your return address but not your company's name on

the envelope flap. If the customer perceives that the "invitation" is from a business, there is less chance that he or she will open it.

3.　Hand address all the envelopes. If you use a typed label or print addresses with a laser printer, you'll signal that the "invitation" is fake. You can probably hire students or even the seniors at a retirement center to do the hand addressing for you.

4.　Use a real stamp, not a bulk-permit number or postage meter. For maximum impact, mail the "invitations" first-class. The ideal stamp is the "LOVE" stamp that is issued every spring for use by brides-to-be on their wedding invitations. Your next choice would be any colorful commemorative stamp. You can make a little extra impact if you can find a stamp that has a relationship to your product or service. For example, a florist could use flower stamps, a car dealer could use antique-car stamps, a movie theater or video store could use showbiz-personality stamps, a sporting goods store could use Olympic Games stamps, and so on. It's a nice touch, but not critical.

For larger mailings, you could use first-class presort, which will save you postage costs, but which limits the types of stamps you can use. The same is true for a third-class mailing. You might want to test these variations and see if using full-price commemorative stamps prompts significantly more responses for you than the less-expensive postage rates.

Other Attention-Getting Mailers

New Arrival

If the information inside the envelope is cleverly done, it can make a big impact. Marc Slutsky's wife, Edye, is a pharmaceutical representative for Squibb and is responsible for Capoten® (a hypertension drug), Pravachol® (a cholesterol-reducing drug), and Duricef® (a broad-base antibiotic). She continued to call on her doctor clients throughout her pregnancy, right up to the day she went into labor. After the delivery she sent out a birth announcement to the doctors incorporating the names of the three drugs she sells. (see Figure 8–3). It prompted a lot of positive comments from her doctors, while also putting those three product names in front of them one more time.

FIGURE 8–3

This mailer got noticed.

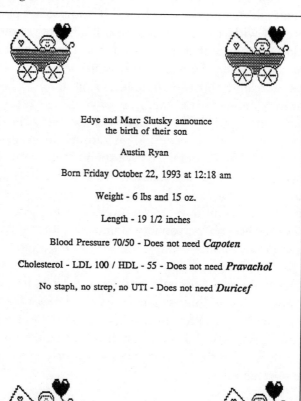

> Edye and Marc Slutsky announce
> the birth of their son
>
> Austin Ryan
>
> Born Friday October 22, 1993 at 12:18 am
>
> Weight - 6 lbs and 15 oz.
>
> Length - 19 1/2 inches
>
> Blood Pressure 70/50 - Does not need *Capoten*
>
> Cholesterol - LDL 100 / HDL - 55 - Does not need *Pravachol*
>
> No staph, no strep, no UTI - Does not need *Duricef*

Before Marc and Edye ran off their "birth announcement" on my laser printer at the office, Edye talked to the pediatrician to get the real vital signs and terminology that would be used in the flier. The entire flier was copied on light-blue paper and mailed in a standard Squibb envelope. Despite its standard appearance, the piece got opened and was noticed.

Marriage Mailers

Some companies provide a group mailing service, the most commonly known of which is Valpak®. Many businesses have reported very good response with these programs. The cost is usually very reasonable, around 4–5¢ each in quantities of ten thousand. That price includes your printing costs for a one-third sheet (8 1/2 x 3 1/2) inserted in a #10 custom-window envelope, postage costs, and the mailing list. Your piece will be one of many, most of which offer some kind of coupon or discount. Larger pieces are also available, as are extra colors and two-sided printing, for additional costs. It helps to vary the offers you do in these group mailings so that your customers don't come to expect the same thing each time.

Some companies promote products and services to new residents, in particular, new home buyers. Welcome Wagon®, one such company, will, for a fee, introduce a newcomer to your product. But Welcome Wagon® generally requires you to supply a free item or a free service. The disadvantage of this service is the high cost for you. The advantage is that it is well targeted. The company's representative shows up in-person to greet the new arrivals and hand out the offers to people who are new to the community and who have yet to choose their dry cleaner, bookstore, or delicatessen. Clients and readers have sent me mixed reviews on this service. My suggestion is to try it out for a few months and see if the results you get justify the costs. You might try working with other companies that can reach this same group using a standard cross-promotion.

Some mailing services can put your offer, solo, right into those new houses or apartments. One such company is C.P.C Associates in Bala Cynwyd, Pennsylvania.[5] This company handles the development, printing, and mailing of pieces to highly targeted lists of potential customers. Costs will depend on quantity and whether the mailing is local or long-distance, and can range from 51¢ to 99¢ per piece. Once you start the program it is completely turn-key. The certificate has the resident's name right on it for maximum impact (see Figure 8–4). You don't have to think about your mailings again unless you want to change your offer. Again, since there is cost involved, you'll have to evaluate this service in terms of the return you get.

Good Fortune

Another mailer that is hard to ignore is custom fortune cookies from Fortunately Yours in Gahanna, Ohio,[6] just down the street

FIGURE 8-4

This company mails your letter and a coupon to all new residents in your neighborhood.

San Francisco Chronicle

FOUR WEEKS FREE!
Sign up for 8 weeks ... Only pay for 4!
That's only $1.35 per week!*
OFFER EXPIRES SOON

Mr. John A. Doe
33 Rock Hill Road
Bala Cynwyd, PA 19004-3119

0592000164 N522 L   DHM

☐ **YES!** Sign me up for 8 weeks of The Chronicle for the price of 4!

CALL
1-800-CHRONICLE
and ask for the new neighbor rate.

_____
DAYTIME PHONE

*Subscription offer good only where Chronicle home delivery is available. Offer void to current subscribers.

Prices may be higher in designated areas. You will be billed for the difference. Chronicle billing is in 8-week cycles.

Good Morning ... and Good News!

Mr. John A. Doe
33 Rock Hill Road
Bala Cynwyd, PA 19004-3119

Dear Mr. Doe:

The San Francisco Chronicle welcomes you to the neighborhood!

We know how difficult moving can be. So, as our way of saying hello, we're offering you your first housewarming gift ... a trial subscription to The Chronicle. Our "8-weeks-for-the-price-of-4" New Neighbor rate will let you try home delivery of The Chronicle for half the regular price.

Daily, you will get world-class news and business coverage and the Sporting Green. Wake up to some of the country's best columnists, Herb Caen and Art Hoppe; sports with Bruce Jenkins, Lowell Cohn and Glenn Dickey; business with Herb Greenberg.

Always on Sunday -- you'll get our Sunday best. The Sunday Examiner & Chronicle combine the best comics and columnists, and the best entertainment features with the award winning main news, sports, and business sections, and Datebook -- Northern California's entertainment guide.

Let us help you get settled in now. Just take a minute to fill out and mail your Chronicle coupon today in the postage-paid envelope enclosed. Or, just call us at 1-800-CHRONICLE.

We look forward to having you as a new neighbor and know you will enjoy receiving The Chronicle at your new home.

Sincerely,

Steven B. Falk
Circulation Director
San Francisco Chronicle

P.S. Act quickly! This offer expires soon.

San Francisco Chronicle

(A)522-05

FIGURE 8–5
This series of three mailers got the sales force in the front door.

from our offices. Rhonda Lashen, the company's founder, provides companies with a unique premium to mail out to their customers. One campaign done for a major pharmaceutical company was intended to remind doctors of the benefits of the company's best-selling prescription drug. Lashen shipped thirteen thousand boxes of fortune cookies the first week. Then she repeated the same mailing to the same list two more times more at one-week intervals so that each doctor's office would receive a total of three mailing.

Each box contained five fortune cookies with custom fortunes about the product's benefits, for example, "Confucius Say: Patients Prescribed (Name of Drug) Enjoyed 38% Lower Costs for Follow-Up Care," and the drug company's logo. Each of the three boxes was centered around a different theme—health, wealth, and happiness—and the fortunes reinforced these themes (see Figure 8–5). Drug information was also enclosed.

The container the cookies came in looked like those used for Chinese food carryout. The goal of the mailing was to have the recipient send back a postcard requesting a sample of the drug, which of course required the pharmaceutical company's representative to visit the doctor. The results were outstanding. The first mailing of

13,000 got a whopping 4,047 responses. The second mailing produced 3,091 responses, third 2,576 responses. That's 9,714 responses from a total mailing of 39,000 pieces, for a response rate of 24.9 percent

Free Mailers

Just as with a cross-promotion, try to find another promotional partner who would be willing to insert your advertising piece in his or her mailers, for free. Consider putting some kind of promotional piece in with your bills when you pay them. The person who handles your vendors' receivables might need what you have. After all, you are his or her customer, and you've already paid for the stamp and the envelope.

Try to get your pieces inserted in the billing and promotional mailings of other businesses, especially your own vendors' mailings. I was able to do a national-level mailing to a highly targeted group. I market *Smart Tele-Selling*, a three-cassette album with a workbook. It teaches how to effectively sell over the phone, primarily business-to-business. In trying to figure out who I could share promotion with to sell this album, it occurred to me that anyone using telemarketing or client-contact database software might be a good prospect. So I contacted the people at TeleMagic. I use this software in my office and I've recommended it in past books and seminars.

I convinced the people at TeleMagic that it would be to their advantage to provide each of their software buyers with a certificate good for a $10 savings on the $59.95 list price of my album, compliments of TeleMagic. They agreed to insert my piece in each of their boxes of software. They asked for five thousand per quarter plus an additional one thousand for a mailing to their resellers. This direct-mail campaign cost me nothing except the printing of the one-third sheet promotional piece. If I had done this mailing on my own, it would have cost me a fortune.

Business-Card Mailing

Sometimes it is not *what* you mail but *why* you mail that gets the customer's attention. When a stylist at an upscale hair salon moved

FIGURE 8–6

This was inserted and shipped in 5,000 telemarketing software boxes and 1,000 mailers, free. Very targeted.

Compliments Of TeleMagic

SAVE $5
Street Smart TeleSelling

The bearer of this certificate is entitled to a $5.00 savings on the purchase of *Street Smart TeleSelling: The 33 Secrets.* Cannot be combined with any other special or savings. Only one certificate per person. Cash value 1/20 cent. Expires in 30 Days. Available from Streetfighter Marketing. 614/337-7474. 800-758-8759. Fax 614/337-2233. Visa, MC, Amex accepted.

---

to a different salon in another part of town many of his customers followed him but eighteen didn't. He started a direct-mail campaign to win them back. He started by mailing each one his new business card; on the back he wrote, "I miss you." Several called and made appointments. During the course of the next year he constantly mailed out remainders to his remaining "lost" customers. He sent birthday and anniversary cards. He sent articles clipped from fashion magazines about new hair-styling techniques. He sent color brochures for new products. He sent cards on the holidays. At the end of the twelve months, he had wooed back all eighteen of his lost customers. Keeping in touch pays.

A Preferred-Customer List

The mailings that get noticed most are the ones requested by the customer himself or herself. Many stores have a preferred-customer list that is generated by asking customers if they want to be included in the list. One successful retail furniture store, Belaire's Comfortime Furniture, developed a list of over ten thousand customers. According to the store's owner, Craig Belaire, that special-customer mailing list is his most important advertising asset.

When Belaire plans a sale, he begins by announcing it to his existing customers through a mailing. This gives his regular customers first shot at the sale-priced merchandise. After these customers have enjoyed their "courtesy days," Belaire announces his sale to the general public via newspaper and radio ads. The combination of direct mailings to his regular customers and mass-media ads works great for him. The mass media reinforces the sale message for all the people who got the mailer. At the same time, the mass-media advertising brings in new customers who then are invited to add their names to the special-mailing list.

Maintaining the list is very important. At least once a year Belaire mails a piece via first-class mail so he can get the returns of those recipients who have moved. This allows him to update his list and keep it current.

The Mailing List

Sometimes the list you mail to is more important than the mailer itself. With the right list you have a much easier chance of getting a response to your mailer. Charlie Willar has a part-time career as Chuckles the Clown and entertains at children's parties. Most of his customers are the parents of five and six year olds who want to have a clown at their kid's birthday party. Willar decided he wanted to get a list of all those children in his vicinity who would be turning five or six in the near future.

To accomplish this, he went the local daily newspaper to visit the "morgue" where all the past issues are stored. He looked up all the birth announcements from five and six years earlier and jotted down the names and addresses. He then mailed a flier offering his services, along with a personalized cover letter introducing himself, to all the addresses on his list. Result? A lot of new customers!

Your most valuable mailing list is your own customer list. The second most important list consists of those who have visited your store but who just didn't buy anything, for whatever reason. Another important list would be that of a competitor's customers. But how could you get your hands on such a list? One way is to record the license numbers of the customer cars parked in that competitor's parking lot. In some states you can write the department of motor vehicles to request the addresses that match license numbers. There is usually a charge involved for this Service, so it can be expensive. But if you sell big-ticket items, such as sports cars, in a very competitive market, it could be worth the expense to generate a list of your rival's costomers.

If you want to get the list of a competitor's customers, you have to ask yourself, "How could someone attempt to get control of my list?" One way they may try is by working with some other business sets up a free drawing at your place of business. For example, you may see display boxes requesting you to fill out a form and drop it in the box to win free health-club memberships or a free cruise. They look harmless enough, and the offered prizes are given away. Obviously, the health club or travel agency will then use those entries to create a mailing or call list to drum up new business. But what happens to those leads when the health club or travel agency is done with them? What if your competitor got his hands on them? Be careful. I always suggest that you never let anyone hold a free drawing at your business unless you control the box of entries.

You might consider buying a list through a list broker. A place to start is with SRDS (Standard Rates and Data Service). It lists about every list you can imagine, who to contact to rent the list, and how much it will cost you. For instance, you can rent lists of association members, magazine subscribers, people who have purchased products via direct response, and thousands more. You can further target those lists to specific Zip Codes. Massive direct-mail campaigns can be very expensive, and there are many variables that effect the response you'll get. You might consider talking to a direct mail expert in your community or at least reading some books that address this topic in greater detail.

Chapter Summary

Direct-mail advertising is one medium that allows you to target a very specific audience. The problem with direct-mail advertising is that only a very small percentage of people who receive mail advertising actually read it. To increase your opportunity of getting noticed through the mail, picture postcards and mailers that look like invitations help. The most important mailing list you can own is the one listing your own customers. The second most important list is your competitor's customers.

Mailers sent in envelopes are more easily ignored, but you can increase your impact by using first-class postage instead of third-class bulk postage, a stamp instead of a permit number or meter, a typed address instead of a label, the recipient's name instead of "Occupant," and handwritten instead of typed addresses.

9

Inbound Telephone
Opportunities

When customers call to inquire about your products or services, you have an opportunity to convert their interest into sales if you know how to effectively handle those calls. Many businesses can't actually make a sale over the phone unless they are a direct-response company that takes credit-card orders. So, for many businesses, the best they can hope to achieve over the phone is to create enough interest so that the prospective buyer is willing to pay them a visit or let them pay him or her a visit. The more expensive the product or service that you offer, or the more involved the customer's decision-making process is, the more you need a strategy to handle telephone opportunities for sales. If you sell such things as cars, RVs, home improvements, self-improvement lessons, specialized services, and high-cost electronics, you should have three major goals for an inbound inquiry:

1. Qualify the caller.
2. Get a commitment for the next contact.
3. Capture the caller's name and phone number.

If time and style permit, you also want to get an address and find out which advertising medium or referral prompted the call. For less-costly items and those services that are easily understood by the caller and therefore require less description (for example, books, video rentals, a car wash, or a manicure), you can use a simplified version of this list. In this case you only need to qualify and to get the commitment. The name and phone number are less important, but they still have value to you. For all inbound inquiries, you want to capture the customer's name so you can add that person to your database for further promotion.

Gaining Control of the Conversation

Before you can achieve your three goals with an inbound inquiry you first have to gain control of the conversation. To gain control you have to ask questions instead of just answering them. Most inbound inquiries have to do with price and availability, so your caller will likely ask you about one or both of these. And as soon as you give him or her an answer the caller has all the information he or she requires and usually thanks you and hangs up, never to be heard from again. The caller, in that instance, is in control because the caller was the one asking all the questions.

Those people who make inbound inquiries are very special people for your database. They're not as valuable as the people in your customer list but they are just below them because even though they haven't visited your business, they have taken the time to call you. They've made the effort to find your phone number from your advertising, cross-promotions, community involvement, publicity, or the Yellow Pages, and have called. Your objective is to convert that caller into a buyer.

When you get an inbound call the caller usually asks you a question like, "Do you sell the Novell NE 2000?" or "How much is it to reserve a room for tonight?" The Streetfighter immediately responds to that kind of question with his or her own question to gain control of the conversation. It doesn't really matter what your first question is because the primary purpose of that first question is to turn the control back over to you. Some logical bounce-back questions might include "When would you be needing it?" or "Is this for yourself?" or "What model will this be used with?" This first question gives you a little information about the customer's needs, but more important, you've regained control of the conversation and you've mentally put yourself in question-asking mode. With a little practice this skill becomes automatic.

A Question of Price

Next you should follow up with more questions to begin your qualifying process. If your caller is asking about a price, you'll eventually have to give the price, but it you give the price immediately you'll lose the caller. So wait to give the price until about the fourth or fifth question. If you wait too long and ask too many questions, the caller will get upset and hang up on you. You have achieve a balance, and this results only from experience.

You'll find it useful at first to work from a survey form or a prompt-sheet so you know what questions to ask. But you don't want to sound like you're reading it; you need to sound totally natural.

Many callers are "letting their fingers do the walking" and comparing your prices with those of your competitors. If you give out a price immediately, you have no idea whether you have earned a shot at the caller's business or not. You don't even know if the price is a fair comparison when your quality and service are considered. So, when you give a price always follow up with a question that reveals the caller's reaction to that price. If your price seems to be too high for the caller, you may have other options to attract him or her.

"The standard project is $5,500. Is that in the ball park?" Or, "They go for between $4,500 and $7,500 depending on the size and the quality of materials. Is that what you had in mind?" Always follow your price quotation with a question to keep you in control and to give you feedback concerning the price you've just presented. If the price seems to be OK for the caller, then ask for the commitment. "Can I put one on hold for you?" or "Let's set up a time to get the paperwork out of the way. Okay?" Once the caller has made a commitment, the likelihood of the caller continuing to call other competitors is greatly reduced.

Qualify the Caller

Qualifying saves you a lot of time and effort. You want to learn enough information about your potential customer as quickly as possible so that you can make an intelligent guess about whether the caller has the potential to buy from you. If the caller can't buy from you, don't waste your time by staying on the phone with him or her. Sometimes callers want you to send them information. Often the prospects who ask for information aren't really seriously interested. So, in your inbound inquiry process you need to have a contingency approach for the "Send information" callers. This allows you to stay on track and finish qualifying.

Printed materials, postage, and handling are expensive, so send information only when you have a reasonable expectation of getting the caller's business.

To qualify your caller you need to ask several questions to find out some important information. There are usually five qualifiers or tests your prospective customer needs to pass before you should make a commitment to pursue the sale. Of course, every type of business is different and you may want to modify my list to suit your particular needs. Use these five qualifiers as your starting point:

1. Need
2. Want
3. Decision Maker
4. Decision Mode
5. Budget (Also includes any money or credit issues)

Need

This is a necessity or a requirement. Need deals more with reality or the perceived reality of the caller's situation. In selling an intangible like life insurance, for example, you could ask the prospect, "Do you need life insurance?" Although this question deals with the prospect's need, you are not likely to get a truly accurate response by using it. The response would be much different if you asked an entirely different question that zeroed in on the "benefit." For example, "How important is it to you to ensure that your family has enough income to live on should you have an unfortunate accident?"

Want

The prospect has to want the benefits of your product or service. If he does not want it, even if he needs it, its very hard to get a sale.

Do not waste your time with a caller unless he or she wants it. If callers want it a great deal, their perception is that they need it.

Decision Maker

The third qualifier is to find out if you are talking to the decision maker. If you aren't, you are wasting your time. If the decision is going to be made by more than one person, then it is vital that you talk to all the decision makers simultaneously if possible. Without talking to the decision maker, you have little chance of closing the sale. The same holds true when only one of several decision makers are present.

Sometimes you may find that you are forced to deal with a *decision influencer*. For example, when a male customer is considering buying a certain product he might not be willing or able to commit until he has his wife's or his business partner's okay. Suggest that you, the influencer, and the decision maker all meet. If that's not possible, then you must first sell the influencer on the value of your product or service, then train the influencer to sell your product or service to the decision maker on your behalf. This complicates the process and should only be used as a last resort.

Don't jump to conclusions about decision makers for large purchases. Many real-estate agents and car dealers have lost sales by assuming that a woman needs to get someone else's approval before making a purchase.

Decision Mode

The fourth qualifier is decision mode. Can your prospective customer make a decision within a certain time? If you're selling copy machines or FAX machines and your prospect just bought one a year ago, you know that he or she probably will not be in a decision-making mode for at least another year unless his or her company is planning an expansion or is not happy with its current equipment.

Perhaps your customer is planning to use her quarterly bonus to pay for a large purchase. The commitment is less likely to be made until that bonus is banked. Knowing your prospect's buying cycle keeps you from trying to close a sale before the customer is ready.

Budget

The fifth qualifier is money-related. Is your prospect willing to spend the money for what you are selling? Do not confuse willingness to spend money with affordability. When someone tells you he cannot afford something, that is his opinion, not necessarily a statement of fact. The prospect is telling you that you have not convinced him or her enough to justify the expenditure.

You have to be careful with the budget qualifier because prospects will often tell you that they can only spend a certain amount of money. But, if you offer them a terrific buy or convince them of the true value of what you have to offer, price fades away as a problem.

Money also has to do with credit. If the customer can't qualify for the financing of the purchase and doesn't have the ready cash, no sale can be made. You want to know this as soon as possible so you don't waste a lot of effort in pursuing a futile prospect.

To Qualify, That's the Question

Here's an example of a situation where the caller is interested in renting an apartment.

OWNER: Thank you for calling Colonial Apartments. How I can I help you?

CALLER: I would like to find out what the rent is on a two-bedroom apartment.

OWNER: Is this for yourself?

CALLER: Yes.

OWNER: And when will you be needing it?

CALLER: My lease is up in a month and a half, so I'd need something within six weeks.

OWNER: I see. And where are you living now?

CALLER: I'm at Lakewood East Apartments, right off Main.

OWNER: Oh yea. I know exactly where they are. By the way, my name is Jeff Slutsky. And who am I speaking to?

CALLER: John Smith.

OWNER: Well John, our two-bedroom apartments range between $400 and $525 a month depending on the size and floor plan. Is that in your budget?

CALLER: Well, it's a little more than I planned on.

OWNER: Just how far off are we, John?

CALLER: Oh, about $25 a month. I've called around.

OWNER: Let me ask you this. Other than the budget, is there any other reason that would keep you from making Colonial your first choice?

CALLER: Not really. Your place is a lot closer to my job. But $25 adds up.

OWNER: I hear you. Let me suggest this. We run specials from time to time. What I'd like to do, with your permission, is to set up a time to have you come out and visit with us and get a real good look at our property. And then look at a couple ways we could fit this in your budget. Would that be fair?

CALLER: Sounds fine to me.

OWNER: Great. First let me get your phone number, John.

CALLER: 337-7474.

OWNER: OK. Now let's look for a time. What's a good day for you this week?

CALLER: Tomorrow's good.

OWNER: I'm sure we can work that out. What's a good time?

CALLER: Oh I don't know, about 3:00.

OWNER: Oooh. Three is booked but I'm available at 3:10. Is that close enough.

CALLER: Sure.

OWNER: Great. And what's your mailing address, John?

CALLER: 467 Waterbury Court.

OWNER: Okay. I got you down for tomorrow at 3:10. And if for some reason you can't make it, just give me a call. OK?

CALLER: No problem.

OWNER: See you tomorrow at 3:10. By the way, how did you hear about us?

CALLER: I drive right by the place every day on the way to work.

OWNER: OK. I'll see you tomorrow at 3:10.

In this example notice that when the caller picked a time for the visit, the owner said he was booked but was available ten minutes later. This maneuver shows the caller that your time is valuable and you're in demand.

Always Be Selling

Bill Ellis of E & E Remodelers in Columbus, Ohio, tells the story of how he got a big window replacement job thanks to a wrong number. He came home beat after a tough day and then the phone rang. "Is Joe there?," the woman on the line asked. "There's no Joe here, but I'm a remodeler. Are you in the market for doing some remodeling in your home?," Ellis asked without missing a beat. The woman answered, "As a matter of fact, we were just talking about replacing our windows." He offered to come right over—which he did. He eventually landed a big sale.

My brother, Marc, uses a similar approach at our office. Whenever he gets a telemarketing call he responds by letting them know that their telephone-selling skills were OK but could stand some improvement. Then he offers to sell them our audio album, *The 33 Secrets of Street Smart Tele-Selling* for $59.95. Most of the callers want to hang up in a hurry. To date he's had one sale from someone who made a personal sales call about copy machines she bought, we didn't.

Chapter Summary

Your goal with an inbound telephone inquiry is to (1) qualify the caller; (2) to get a commitment for a visit; and (3) to capture the name, phone, and address of your caller. You qualify by asking questions about the caller's need, want, decision-making ability, decision mode, and budget.

When you give a price over the phone, always follow up by asking the caller if it's "in his budget" or "in the ball park." The feedback from the caller helps you determine if the sale is worth pursuing.

Keep in mind that this same qualifying process should also be used for those customers who visit you in person. This could be a walk-in at your store or office or could be an appointment you've set up where you visit with him or her in his or her office or home.

10

Outbound Telephone Marketing

The telephone is probably the most underused marketing tool in your business. It's also the only truly interactive marketing medium you have, with the exception of a personal visit. Despite all of the benefits it offers, most businesses don't use the phone to increase their sales.

There are many opportunities to get sales by contacting your customers and potential customers over the phone on a regular basis. Many times you can use outbound telephone calls as a supplement to direct-mail and advertising campaigns. You can use these calls for a more aggressive marketing approach or simply as a reminder of appointments. As I was writing this, I got a phone call from my dentist's office manager. This is the same dentist that sends me a reminder postcard when it is time for a checkup. This time she was reminding me that I had an appointment the next day.

In Chapter 8 you read about a hair stylist who successfully regained eighteen former customers by sending them mailings regularly for twelve months. If he had called them at least once after the first mailing, even just to leave a message on their answering machines, I would guess that he would have gotten them back sooner and without the expense of continually mailing out the reminders and greeting cards.

Reactivating past customers is a powerful use for outbound telephone calls. While I was preparing a seminar for the National Marine Manufacturing Association, I came across a piece of research that said that 8 percent of all existing boat owners, on average, were in the market to buy a new boat in the next twelve-month period. That's a significant number! The average boat dealer's customer base is about one thousand boat owners. In other words, the average boat dealer has about eighty potential new sales per year hidden in his or her database of past customers. The trick is to find out which eighty they are before they decide to buy a new boat somewhere else.

There are a couple of ways to begin your outbound telephone process. One way that works well is the "customer-satisfaction survey" approach. You call your customers and ask their permission to find out how much they liked doing business with you. Later in the survey you also ask questions to determine if they're in the market to buy and what they're looking for. This process creates a qualified-buyers list. Then you invite the qualified buyers into your store or office to take a look at what you have to offer.

This process worked well for Bob Kramer of Kramers Sew & Vac in Cincinnati. He developed his qualified-buyers list from people who attended a sewing clinic at which he was one of the sponsors. Viking Sewing Machines had just come out with a new top-of-the line computerized sewing machine. He wanted to invite the participants from the clinic into his store, but he knew that sewing-machine users are very wary of "demos" because of the high-pressure sales tactics used by many in the industry. He wanted to use a more subtle approach. He also knew that if he could attract customers to his store to try the new machines, they would be so impressed by their quality that he would automatically achieve big sales.

To increase the credibility of his telephone call, he got permission from the manufacturer to use its name along with his own for a "research" project on the new machines. He called the list of participants and said that he was looking for sewers to spend about ten minutes working with the new models and then to fill out a brief survey form to provide feedback about the machines. For their help they would receive a $25 gift certificate to his store. He made twenty-five calls and got five people to visit his store to try the machines. His effort resulted in three sales.

The Outbound Phone Call

The outbound phone call has three stages:

1. The Opener
2. Qualifying and Probing
3. The Call to Action

The Opener

Once you get the decision maker on the line, what do you say? The most critical part of selling over the phone is the first ten or twenty seconds of talking directly with your prospect. There are four parts to a successful telephone opener:

1. Your introduction
2. Your benefit statement
3. The "new" news
4. Permission to pursue

YOUR INTRODUCTION

Step 1 of your "opener" is to introduce yourself and the company you represent. One proven technique as an effective opener is to repeat the prospect's name to make sure you do have the right person on the line. Here is an example of the first line in the opener using this approach:

> "Mr. Herman? [Wait for a response like 'Yes' or 'You've got him.'] Mr. Herman, this is Jeff Slutsky with Streetfighter Marketing in Columbus, Ohio."

In that first sentence, Mr. Herman heard his name twice. He responds to the caller, an act that immediately involves him in the conversation. He knows who the caller is, what company or organization the caller represents, and where the call is coming from. You mention your city if most of your calls are long-distance because it seems to add a sense of urgency and importance by letting your prospect know that he or she is important enough to deserve a long-distance call. However, if you are making a local call, you might consider a slight change, such as: "This is Jeff Slutsky from

Streetfighter Marketing *here* in Columbus." This works best when close proximity is an important feature to your prospect.

YOUR BENEFIT STATEMENT

Since my name or my company's name probably doesn't mean much to Mr. Herman, my second sentence explains in a very precise and concise way the benefits of what I have to offer. A good benefit statement is even more important if your company name is well known. This is because your prospective customer may already think he or she knows the purpose of your call and might try to cut you off before you get an opportunity to present your benefits.

So you immediately launch into the next sentence that explains the benefits of what you do and why you are unique. In my case, I would *not* say "I conduct seminars, workshops, and training projects in neighborhood marketing." That tells Mr. Herman just enough information so he can tell me he has no interest in my phone call.

Instead, stress the unique benefits of your products and services to the prospect. For example, I might say: "We're specialists in the area of helping businesses learn how to advertise, promote, and generally increase sales without spending much money."

Now that is a benefit. Notice that I did not mention anything about seminars or consulting. Those are details. How I do what I say I do is of little consequence. The fact that I offer these benefits or results is the key.

THE "NEW" NEWS

The third sentence should mention the "new" news. You have to have a special reason for the phone call that creates a sense of urgency. It could be a new product or a service you are introducing, or a special introductory offer. You want to provide one more piece of news that "sweetens" the benefit for the prospect. For example, sometimes I say something like, "The reason I'm calling you is because we have recently developed some new techniques that many of our clients tell us are getting them tremendous response."

PERMISSION TO PURSUE

Now I am ready for the fourth and final sentence of my opener, asking permission to continue our discussion. Therefore, the last sentence must be a question. And, since I am asking a question to get permission to do something, it must require a "Yes" or "No" response.

The problem is that the natural reaction of almost anyone who gets anything related to a telephone solicitation is to say "No." They want to say "No." They are conditioned to say "No." They are used to ill-trained scriptreaders calling them up and boring them to death with a pitch like, "Hi. My name is Jeff. How are you doing today? We would like you to buy tickets to the circus. . . ."

As soon as you start, their natural reaction is to say that they have no interest: "No, thanks anyway, but no." Since most of the people you are going to talk to on the phone are already preconditioned to say "No," you have to design the closing of your opener in a way to get them to respond with a "No." In responding with a "No," they actually give an affirmative answer to your question, and therefore permission to continue with the presentation. So, my ending question might be something like, "Is there any reason you wouldn't want to learn a little bit more about it?" The party at the other end answers "No," and then I can go on: "Great! Let me ask you. . . ."

Now you are in the front door. It's that simple. You can change the wording to make it more comfortable for you, and of course you need to find just the right description of who you are and the new news you wish to present to your prospect.

Another approach you might try, depending on the type of product or service you sell, is to add another question in the middle of the opener. But this works only if your company name is not widely known and if giving the name of your company won't deter parties from taking your phone call. The second approach goes like this:

"This is Jeff Slutsky of Streetfighter Marketing. We specialize in teaching businesses how to advertise, market, and generally increase sales without spending a lot of money. We call our unique program 'Streetfighting.' Have you heard of us? Well, as I said, we specialize in teaching low-cost promotional programs intended for the local level, and we have just developed some new techniques that many of our clients report are getting them some great results. Is there any reason you wouldn't want to learn a little bit more about it?"

In this example I sneak in that extra question "Have you heard of us?" This brings the listener into the conversation sooner. The question is useful because every once in a while the party responds with a "Yes." In that case I follow up with something like, "No kidding. How do you know us?" I want to find out what the party knows and whether his or her impression is favorable so I will know how to proceed from there.

Usually, however, the answer is "No." This then gives me an opportunity to repeat and perhaps even refine or expand the benefit statement and then to go on as I normally do. In the example, I added the information that our program is focused on the "local level." Note that I also mentioned both the company name and the product name.

This approach might not be as effective if you are calling on behalf of American Express or AT&T. You wouldn't want to call a prospect and begin by telling him that you are with American Express, "Have you heard of us?" You do not want to insult his intelligence and get off to a bad start.

To give you a better idea of what a good opener is, let's look at some examples. The first is used by a package delivery company. I'll call it Lickety-Split:

> "Mr. Jones? This is Dan Robinson with the Lickety-Split Package Express Service. We specialize in shipping time-sensitive packages on the same day or the next day by 8:30 A.M. We just introduced a new introductory program that allows you to save 60 percent on the cost of shipping with us for the next three months. Is there any reason why you wouldn't want to learn more about it?"

Notice that all four parts of the opener are included: introduction, description of the benefit, new news, and permission to continue.

Of course, you can change the elements in the opener at any time as new developments come up, but be careful not to pigeonhole yourself. For example, you just opened a new market that is "new news." The prospect you call may have no need for this new market, but could benefit from your service in other ways. If you offered "new news" that was too specific, he or she could blow you off. In the Lickety-Split example, for instance, it might be dangerous to use a "new news" sentence like, "We've just started shipping directly to Huntington and Bluffton, Indiana." That gives your prospect the opportunity to respond with, "We never ship to those cities. Thanks anyway. Good-bye."

Make sure that your "new news" is something that won't invite a turndown. It can be any development or enhancement in service, for example, a special price reduction.

A discount motel uses an appropriate opener geared for its particular business. When selling by phone to get corporate accounts, the marketer opens like this:

> "This is Rob Davis with Drive-By Motor Inns here in Columbus. We specialize in providing the highest quality, comfortable motel rooms at very competitive prices. Recently, we've introduced a special corporate discount program that saves you even more money. Is there any reason why you wouldn't want to learn more about it?"

Qualifying and Probing

Whether you want to use the phone to set up an in-person appointment or you want to use the phone for the complete selling process, the next step is the same. The purpose of the qualifying-and-probing stage, whether by phone or in-person, is to discover if the prospect has the potential to buy and, if he or she does, to continue to uncover his or her needs and wants.

Qualifying was discussed in detail in the previous chapter. Probing goes further. One way to uncover the seriousness of the potential customer's needs and wants is to use the "if/then" approach to a trial close. For example, the customer says, "I need a place for my daughter's wedding. We're having about 150 people and want something nice but don't want to spend an arm and a leg. You know what I mean?"

You respond with an answer like this: "Well Mr. Clark, *if* our banquet room could comfortably handle 150 guests and we could do it for a reasonable cost per person, *then* you would want to take advantage of it, *wouldn't* you?"

Call to Action

The last step in your telephone presentation is to ask the prospect to do something. For a major purchase like cars and homes, you want to get ask for a commitment for a visit. For smaller items that could be repeat buys, such as subscription renewals, flowers, books, carpet cleaning, and so on, you want to ask for an order.

The Mail Follow-Up

When selling complicated and competitive services such as insurance, financial products, and consulting and advertising services, you might want to send your prospective customer some information before your face-to-face visit to build familiarity and credibility.

However, there is a danger in doing so: sending information before you visit can allow your prospect to make a decision about your product or service before you visit, that is, before you are on-site to ensure that the prospect makes the "right" decision. Therefore, your initial mail follow-up should be very carefully planned. You should provide prospective customers with just enough information to establish your credibility and excite their curiosity, but not enough so that the prospect can make a decision by himself or herself.

Your mail piece may include your standard company background brochure; publicity you have received from local, national, or trade publications; and biographical information on you. Items that don't belong include technical information and—especially—pricing information. That follows later.

The last element is the cover letter to your prospect. This should be a strong sales letter that reinforces everything you brought out in your phone conversation, and that reminds the prospect about your future appointment when the two of you will talk again. Here's an example of a cover letter I sent to David's Food Stores:

(Date)

Dear David:

It was a pleasure talking to you today about how each of your David's Food Stores can increase sales greatly on a shoestring budget using our effective "Streetfighting" local-store marketing program.

As you know, our "Streetfighting" local-store marketing program has received a great deal of national attention from publications like the

Wall Street Journal, USA Today, and *Inc.* magazine, to name just a few. This unique program could be adopted specifically for your David's Food Stores.

You'll find that our "Streetfighting" program is a welcome addition to your marketing efforts, and each of your David's Food Stores can implement these very effective, easy-to-do sales-building programs.

I look forward to talking to you soon. If you have any questions, feel free to call me anytime. Just dial 1-800-SLUTSKY (800-758-8759).

Best Wishes,

Notice that the letter only reinforces our previous conversation. There is nothing new in the letter, nothing that wasn't discussed in the phone call, nor is there any specific information that the customer could use to back out of our arranged meeting.

Dealing with Procrastinators and Handling Objections

There are generally two types of objections: serious obstacles and delay tactics. Objections are ways in which your prospect delays making a decision. Making an important decision is a very painful process for many people. Even though a prospect may not realize it, discomfort is a common feeling when one is confronted with any kind of significant decision. Therefore, to be rid of this pain, a prospect often attempts to delay the process of decision making.

According to Bill Bishop, a sales trainer based in Orlando, Florida, studies were done at some major universities where subjects were electronically monitored. During the experiments, the subjects were confronted with making some kind of decision. These subjects' brain-wave patterns were remarkably similar to the patterns of other subjects enduring physical pain. Once the subjects made a decision—and it made no difference what choice they made—the painlike brain waves returned to normal.

With procrastinating prospects, it's not only important to demonstrate the benefits of your project, but also the importance of buying your product *now*. You need to create a sense of urgency to get your procrastinator to make a decision.

Price and availability are frequently used to create a sense of urgency. For example, a real estate opportunity could be lost because somebody else is interested in the same property. Stock prices are expected to rise, so your prospect has to act before it is too late. A disaster could happen at any moment, leaving your prospect's family unprotected, so it is imperative that he buy insurance policy immediately. Your prospect's business is losing the increased profits and time-saving benefits associated with use of this computer or telecommunications system, and should have it installed right now.

Your prospects will raise objections, of course. But take them as a good sign. Objections are a way for your prospect to continue to express his interest and also to signal you that you haven't provided enough benefits to allow him to make a positive decision.

Understanding the psychology of decision making can help you to devise an effective strategy for dealing with objections. You need to anticipate objections during your presentation. If a prospect raises an objection, address it during the early stages of your presentation so it doesn't come back to interfere with your close. Use the four-step method of handling objections:

1. Soften
2. Isolate
3. Rephrase
4. Suggest a solution.

Your prospect may have a number of objections tucked away in the back of her head. When you ask her to make a decision, she springs an objection on you. To break the chain-response of having to answer one objection after another, use the four-step process.

Soften

No matter what objection is raised, you respond with a simple "I understand." This response does two things. First, it shows your prospect that, unlike most salespeople, you're not going to jump down her throat when she asks a question. Second, it puts you into an objection-handling mode. With practice, when you respond with "I understand," the next three steps become a reflex action.

Isolate

This step makes it more difficult for the prospect to come back with another objection after the first one is dealt with satisfactorily. You say, "Other than [insert the relevant objection], is there any other reason why we can't get the go-ahead on this order right now?"

If the prospect answers "No," you have learned that this is your prospect's *only* reason for not making a decision now. Notice how this technique encourages your prospect to agree to buy your product or service once this one-and-only objection is dealt with positively.

Also, notice that the marketer avoids using painful sales words like "decision," "sign," or "contract." Instead, the marketer uses expressions such as "go-ahead," "give it a try," or "get the ball rolling." Rather than asking the prospect to "sign," you might ask for her "approval." "Contracts" become the "paperwork." These words and phrases are informal, and consequently make the decision-making process seem less serious.

Remember: anything your prospect says is true in his or her prospect's mind, but anything you say to the prospect is suspect. Therefore, by getting the prospect to agree that a particular objection is the only thing standing between you and the sale, it becomes very difficult for the prospect to come back with another objection.

Rephrase

The third technique is to rephrase your prospect's objection so that you can answer it positively. For example, if your prospect says, "I can't afford it," you might respond "If I understand you correctly, Mary, it costs too much. Is that your question?" Even though she didn't ask a question, refer to her objection as if she did. Once the prospect admits that it costs too much (instead of a blanket "I can't afford it"), you can narrow her objection down to how much she *can* afford.

Also note that in this example the statement of "affordability" was converted to a question of "cost." This is done because affordability is an opinion and you cannot address an opinion. Cost, on the other hand, is a price/value relationship that can be addressed.

Suggest a Solution

Once affordability is rephrased into a question of cost, the next question you would ask is, "How much too much?" So if you've priced your product or service at $1,000 and Mary thinks it's over-priced, you need to find out by how much so you can deal with it. If she doesn't respond right away with a lower price, you prompt her by offering three price points, thinking that she'll most likely choose the last one. It would sound like this, "Is it $50 too much, $100 too much, $150 too much?"

Let's say she chooses $150 too much. She's just told you that $150 stands between you and the sale. You are no longer talking about $1,000. You have to show her enough value to warrant her spending the extra $150.

Closing the Sale

Here's where you make your money. Everything up to now leads to this point. If you followed all the key points and steps prior to the close, this will be the easiest part of the sale.

One of the first rules is that you must ask for the order. If you don't ask, you don't get! It's as simple as that! The following true story illustrates this point. The owner of a large printing company was the friend of a bank president. The two played golf together every week for thirteen years. One day the owner of the printing company said, "Dave, we have been playing golf together for years. How come you never use my printing company?" The bank president responded, "You never asked me."

One other key point to keep in mind is that it takes numerous (perhaps six or more) attempts before you get to "Yes." Most sales-people quit after just one or two attempts. Yet, if you are persistent and continue to handle all objections, probe further, ask more questions, and keep asking for the order, you will dramatically increase your sales production.

Closing the sale is similar to baseball. For instance, only a top batter hits in the .300 range. But to bat .300 he strikes out or is put out seven out of ten times. Babe Ruth hit more home runs than anybody, but he also held the record for most strikeouts.

To close, you have to get the prospect to say "Yes." To get someone to say "Yes," you have to ask a question that requires a "Yes" or "No" response, as opposed to one asking for an opinion. For example, you do not ask, "What do you think?" The prospect can easily respond with, "Sounds pretty good, but I want to think about it."

After addressing an objection or even a question, try to turn it into a close. For example, the prospect might ask, "How long will it take to get delivery?" This red flag tells you that the prospect wants to buy. You will lose a great opportunity for a close if you answer, "Oh, we can get it to you as early as next week." That kind of answer allows the prospect to respond, "Great, I'll get back to you."

Learn to respond to a question with a question. For example, for the question "How long will it take to get delivery?," you could reply, "When would you like to take delivery?" For the question "Can I get it delivered next Tuesday?," you could reply, "Would you like delivery on Tuesday?" When you get a "Yes," you then respond, "I'll put you down for a Tuesday delivery." The sale is made.

The prospect might ask, "Does it come in blue?" You respond, "Do you want it in blue?" Another prospect says, "Can I get it with low monthly installments?" And you fire back, "Do you want low monthly installments?"

What if blue is not available or you don't have low monthly installments to offer? Then you need to see how serious that objection is by asking, "How important is it to you to get it in blue?" If it's not important you go forward.

In every case, if he or she responds with "Yes," you go for the magic close. From that point, assume the sale is made, and reinforce it by asking for a check, a credit-card number, or something else to cement the deal.

Remember: sales is a numbers game. The more people you contact, the more sales you'll make. Therefore, to get the maximum number of appointments or orders from your Streetfighter selling efforts, you must look for every possible way to make the best use of your time. *The only time you're making money is when you're on the phone selling or in the client's presence selling!* You don't make money doing paperwork, filling orders, filing reports, running errands, or looking for leads. You make money only when you're selling on the phone and then following up these phone calls. Obviously, you have to know whom you're going to call, what you're going to say, and how you're going to keep track of your progress. However, you don't make any money directly even when you're doing these important tasks.

Tracking

Don't waste valuable telephone selling time looking up numbers that should have been found ahead of time. If your peak selling hours are between 9:00 A.M. and 5:00 P.M., you want to spend as much of that time as possible on the phone. If it takes an hour a day for you to get organized, be at your office at 8:00 A.M. or stay late—but don't waste your valuable selling time.

If you have a secretary or an assistant to whom you can delegate these tasks, that's even better. Your time could be worth $25, $40, or $100 an hour when you're selling, but it is only worth minimum wage when you're doing grunt work. Hire someone to do the grunt work so you can spend more time making money.

After each phone call, record important points about the prospect. Develop special tracking sheets (for an example, see Figure 10–1) that help you to recall vital information easily, without wasting time by writing detailed notes after each call. By using them, you'll spend less than a minute after each call instead of five or ten precious selling minutes.

Valuable tracking information you want to know is:

1. Number of total dials you made on the phone
2. Number of sales presentations made to decision makers
3. Number of appointments made
4. Number of orders
5. Length of time of each presentation.

These are just a few statistics, but these numbers help you fine-tune your organizational skills so you spend more valuable selling time actually selling.

By utilizing this type of valuable information, you'll soon be able to discover opportunities that increase your sales results. For example, you may have a lot of dials but few conversations. This tells you that you need to work on your opener. If you have a lot of conversations but very few appointments, you need to work on your

FIGURE 10–1
Tracking your phone calls gives you valuable information about your efforts.

RMI DAILY TELEPHONE LOG SHEET

Date_____   Salesperson _____   Total Dials _____

8:00										
9:00										
10:00										
11:00										
12:00										
1:00										
2:00										
3:00										
4:00										
5:00										
6:00										
7:00										
Total										

close. If you set up a lot of appointments but are getting very few closes, you need to qualify better.

You can use your tracking sheet to help you understand the best times to make sales telephone calls for your type of business. On the tracking sheet, color in the box with a black marker for the time periods that you think are your prime selling time. Then go back and place a large "X" through those days and time periods that are mediocre calling times.

There are also numerous time-saving devices to help keep you selling more during your peak time. Consider getting computer contact management software. It does everything for you, including dialing the phone. An efficient program will find any prospect or customer you've encoded in your computer by the company name, the contact's name, or even his or her phone number. You use the computer to make a variety of form letters that automatically merge customers' names and addresses into the letter for you, as well as address the envelope or label. The bottom half of the computer screen has a notepad where you can document all your conversations. The recall date provides you with an automatic "tickler" file so you will be sure to follow up when you're suppose to.

Computers and specialized software will enable you to do all sorts of customized mailings to your customers, indexed any way you want. A computer can easily double your productivity. (If you have more than one computer, you'll want to network your computers so each user is working off the same database.)

If you're not computerized, you could use a speed dialer to help you plan your calling and keep you on track. If you want to make twenty-five calls per day, you preprogram those twenty-five numbers into your speed dialer the day before. The next day you simply sit down at your desk and start with the first speed-dialed number and work your way through the list.

Let's say you managed to reach ten of your prospective twenty-five customers for that day. Replace those ten numbers with ten new ones for the next day. You keep the fifteen numbers you didn't reach because you still need to reach them. They stay in the speed dialer until you've gotten a "Yes" or a "No," or you've called so many times it's not worth pursuing that one prospect any longer.

Telephone-recording devices allow you to hear and review your actual presentation after you've made it. Such review helps you improve your presentation, voice clarity, inflection, objection handling, and other aspects of your Streetfighter teleselling activities. There is nothing like hearing your presentation after the fact to open your eyes to ways to achieve more effective selling.

Another item that helps a lot with calling is a good-quality headset. A headset allows you to keep you hands free for taking notes. When you're on the phone for an hour straight, you'll find that you'll get less fatigued if you don't have to hold on to the receiver. Don't skimp. Buy a headset that is comfortable and has good sound quality.

When using a handset, however, George Walther, author of *Phone Power* and *Power Talking* suggests that you use a twenty-five-foot coil cord so you're not tied to your desk. It gives you the freedom to move around.

More from the Floor

If you have salespeople who traditionally "work the floor" you should incorporate an outbound-telephone-sales program. No owner of a business dealership (whether for cars, boats, RVs, appliances, electronics, or whatever) should allow salespeople to sit around reading magazines, waiting for customers to show up. During down-times the sales representatives should be calling past customers or shoppers. Even if they do nothing except call those customers who bought three to twelve months earlier just to ask how the item is working and getting feedback from that customer, their calls will generate additional interest in future sales.

In addition to your existing customers and people who have been to your business to inquire about your products, you should also call interested prospects. For example, if you exhibit at a local trade show, capture the names of anyone who visits your booth and shows interest. You can easily do that with a free drawing.

One simple telephone program was used by a savvy auto-body-shop owner. Whenever he was out at a mall and noticed a car that was damaged, he would leave his business card on the windshield with a note asking the owner to call him for a good price on fixing the car. He would then jot down the license number of the car and for $1 get the name and address of the car's owner from the department of motor vehicles. If there was no response to the windshield card, he went to phase two and sent out a mail piece. If that didn't get a response within a week, he'd initiate phase three and call the prospect.

The key to success in outbound calls is consistency. You need to make the effort on a regular basis. You set aside a specific time period every week for making your calls. Or you determine to make a certain number of calls every day or every week. The number isn't all that important; what is important is that phone marketing becomes part of your regular operation.

One other use for outbound calls is as an alternative or a supplement to a specialized mailer (mentioned in Chapter 8). In your database you should have the key information about a customer, including birthday, anniversary, spouse's name and birthday, children's names and birthdays, and preferences regarding the products and services you offer. Ahead of key gift-giving times you could send the customer a postcard, but a phone call is faster and gives you an opportunity to do some selling and get an order over the phone. The more expensive the item you sell, the more I would recommend a phone call instead of a mail piece.

Chapter Summary

The telephone is a powerful proactive marketing tool. The outbound phone call has three stages: (1) opener; (2) qualifying and probing, and (3) call to action. When you first make contact, use a benefit statement and end with a question to get the interest of the prospect. Then ask some qualifying questions to determine need, want, decision maker, decision mode, and budget. Once qualified, get the prospect to make a commitment to visit with you.

When the prospect offers an objection, determine if it serious. If it is, use the four-step process for dealing with objections: (1) soften; (2) isolate, (3) rephrase, and (4) offer a solution. Tracking telephone activity helps you gage your efficiency and guide you to areas of the selling process that need improvement. Using a computer and contact management software is a big time-saver. Get salespeople to use their down-time to contact past customers and prospects.

11

Print Advertising

Print advertising is one of the oldest and most prevalent forms of advertising. Most large markets have at least one daily newspaper and some weekly specialty papers for example, an arts and entertainment journal, a real estate journal, community newspapers, and the like. In addition to newspapers, there might be some local magazines and buyers guides. Your market might even have some national publications that have regional or even local editions. In this chapter you'll read about each of these opportunities.

The Daily Newspaper

The typical daily newspaper is a monolopy operation with a strong circulation in the local marketplace. Since it faces little direct competition, it sets it own ad rates and usually doesn't allow haggling unless you're buying lots of ad space each year. Newspaper advertising is very expensive, yet there may be times that you can make such advertising cost-effective for you.

Newspaper Display Ads

AD COPY

The most important part of your ad copy is the headline. It has to grab the attention of the reader by offering some benefit. According to *Olgilvy on Advertising* by David Olgilvy, seven times as many people read the headline as read the body of an ad. So if you want to make sure that your headline attracts the attention of potential customers so they'll look for more detail in your ad.

A benefit headline could be as simple as announcing a big sale or as complex as announcing a brand-new service. Words that you may want to incorporate into your headline include: *discover, free, easy, new, results, you, guarantee, safe, health, money, save,* and *sale.* These words tend to get the reader's attention.

For most local types of businesses, you probably *don't* want to put the name of your business in your headline. There's no benefit to it. If the reader has interest, he or she will find your company name at the bottom of the ad.

You may also want to include a locator in your ad to make it easier to find you (your street address is often meaningless to the potential new customer). Refer to a landmark: "One block south of Main next to Wal-Mart." If a map would be appropriate and you have room for it in your ad, you may want to include that too.

One copy item that you do *not* want to include is "Look for our ad in the Yellow Pages." This phrase should *never* appear anywhere in your advertising: not in your newspaper ads, not in radio or TV ads, not even in billboard ads or on the sides of your company's delivery trucks. Why spend a lot of money getting people to see your ad and then refer them to the only advertising medium that puts your business in the midst of ads from all your major competitors? You may have a great Yellow Pages ad, you may be very proud of it, but you want the Yellow Pages ad to do its own work for you.

NEWSPAPER AD PLACEMENT

If you have a small budget for newspaper ads, you really have very little clout with the newspaper, but you can request placement. Newspapers are usually pretty good about putting your ad in the section of the paper you want, though they usually won't even guarantee that. A daily newspaper has different sections, each of which tends to attract different types of readers, though there are certainly crossovers between sections. For example, the "Sports" section attracts a heavily male readership though more and more women turn to "Sports" these days, thanks to their increasing participation in all kinds of sports. By the same token the "Style" section attracts far more women than men. The Sunday paper gives you a wider selection of sections.

Sunday issues have greater readership than the daily issues, but ad space in Sunday issues costs more and Sunday issues contain many more ads that you will have to compete with. But readers do have a tendency to spend more time with the Sunday paper. You may find that Sunday works best for you unless your ad is time-sensitive, that is, when you are working with an event and a deadline.

Advertise in the sections that are most likely to be read by your customers. If you're selling a lot of RVs to retired couples, you might want to place your ad close to the obituaries (older people are more likely to read the obituaries). Automotive items sell well in the "Sports" section, but should also be advertised in other sections that have a broader readership.

Requesting exact placement within a section usually doesn't work. You'll probably get what the newspaper ad people want to give you. The ideal place is the back page of a section, but that space is usually reserved for a full-page ad, probably with color, and probably with an advertiser who buys full pages on a regular basis. You can make specific requests, but don't expect much satisfaction.

AD SIZE

Newspaper printed-page depths generally vary between 21 and 22 1/2 inches, according to *Newspaper Rates & Data*.[7] An ad 21 inches deep should fit most newspapers and takes into account space at the top for the header. The width of the newspaper is usually expressed in columns. The vast majority of newspapers are six columns wide but there are a few with a little as four columns or as many as nine. You buy advertising space in either column inches or agate lines. There are fourteen lines to a column inch. The larger the ad, the more the cost. The cost of a quarter-page ad is exactly half the cost of a half-page ad, which is half the cost of a full-page ad. Some quantity discounts, based on total space used, are available. An nondiscounted rate is called the "open rate." If you agree to buy a certain amount of space for a year, you then qualify for the discount. If you don't end up buying enough space to justify that discount, you'll receive a "short rate" bill which is based on the difference between what you paid (at the discounted rate) and what you should have paid (based on your actual usage).

The challenge for the Streetfighter Marketer is to create the smallest ad possible that will still do the job. A half-page ad attracts a certain amount of "readership," that is, a percentage of the people who read the newspaper who will actually pay attention to your ad. Those percentages can vary greatly, but for the sake of illustration, let's assume that a typical half-page ad attracts 15 percent readership in your market. If the total circulation of the paper is one hundred thousand, then fifteen thousand people will actually glance at your ad. An even smaller percentage of those fifteen thousand glancers will actually read the ad.

If you reduced that ad from half-page size to quarter-page size, how much readership would you loose? The numbers vary, but the answer is less than half. You'll probably find that the readership drops by 20–25 percent. So you may find that running two quarter-page ads in two different sections or perhaps in the same section on two different days in the same week might attract a stronger readership than the one half-page ad.

But readership is only one part of the equation. There is also the issue of impact. The bottom line with any ad is: Does it bring in the customers? Do they call or visit your business? If you make your ad too small, you may gain readership as a percentage of cost, but you may also loose impact. Was the ad large enough to present enough benefits to cause the reader to take action? The balance of "reach" (the amount of readers who see the ad) versus "frequency" (the number of times the same readers read the ad) is one of the most difficult challenges for businesses on limited ad budgets to surmount.

AD TESTING

Testing is something that is often a function of budget. If you only can afford a two-column (5" wide) by 5" tall ad, then debate is meaningless. And if that 5" x 5" ad works, you know you have something that is successful. But what happens if you increase that ad to three columns, or 7". Does it pull better to the point of justifying the additional cost? Unfortunately, the only way to really know is trial and error.

AD TRACKING

Whenever you advertise, regardless of the medium, you need an indication as to what is working for your business. One way is to simply ask customers "How did you hear about us?" when they call or visit your business. This kind of survey is not scientific or accurate beyond doubt, but it can provide you with a "gut-level" feeling about whether your ads are working.

A more accurate way to test the response of print advertising is to put a coupon that has some value in the ad. Your redemptions will then tell you what kind of response the ad has prompted. Even if you don't ordinarily use coupons, sometimes it's a good idea to to use them just to get a redemption count as a check on the effectiveness of your ads.

To demonstrate how the coupon test works, I will compare two ads selling the same items, both of which contain a coupon. The first ad is a two-column by 5" ad that cost $1,000. The second is a three-column by 5" ad that cost $1,500. The first ad brings in 100 coupons, the second ad brings in 125 coupons. Which is a more effective ad? In this situation, even though the more expensive ad did bring in more responses, the less expensive ad was actually more cost-effective. Looked at from a "cost-per-inquiry" basis, the first cost you $10 per redemption, while the second ad cost you $12 per redemption. You'd be better off running the smaller ad and perhaps running it more often.

Another approach might be to take the difference in the cost of the ads and use it to buy radio spots that specifically ask the listener to look for your ad in a particular issue of the local paper.

Or let's go back to the same two example ads. For $3,000 you could buy three of the $1,000 ads but only two of the $1,500 ads. If the redemption numbers hold up during this ad campaign, the first approach would bring you in 300 redemptions versus 250 for the second approach. Again, the smaller ad would be more cost-effective.

STREETFIGHTER AD-PLACEMENT STRATEGIES

The Streetfighter's Cheater Page. Given a limited budget, you usually don't want to buy a full-page ad in your local daily paper unless

FIGURE 11–1

A: Full-page 6 col x 21"; B: Cheater's Page 5 col x 18"; C: Dominator Page 4 col x 14".

you can get special placement like on the back page of a section. Instead, you might try out the "Streetfighter's Cheater's Page" (see B in Figure 11–1). You buy an ad that is located three to four inches below the top of the page and sized one column less than full width. In a six-column paper, the ad would be five columns by eighteen inches in size—still a very large ad. You should get nearly the same readership with a full-page ad, yet you're saving thirty-six column inches. In a six-column paper, a full-page is 126 column inches. You save nearly 36 percent of the total ad space, which translates into 36 percent of the total cost of that ad. If a full-page ad costs $10,000, you save over $3,500.

The Streetfighter's Dominator Page. The next type of ad goes one step further. I call this the Streetfighter's Dominator Page (see C in Figure 11–1). This ad is located three to four inches above the center fold of the newspaper. The center fold is at ten inches, so you run an ad that is fourteen inches tall. The width is one column more than half. In a six-column paper, the ad would be four-column by fourteen inches in size. No other ad on the page can be larger than yours. Your ad will get noticed. This ad would take up fifty-six column inches, but would cost less than half the cost of a full-page ad.

AD LAYOUT CONSIDERATIONS

It would probably be wise to use a good commercial layout artist to design your ad. You want the ad to look professional and clean, but you don't want it cluttered up with a lot of artwork that has no meaning. If you use an illustration or photograph, it should have meaning to the reader. Illustrations take up a lot of expensive space.

Generally, photographs make a stronger impression than line drawings, but line drawings reproduce better in newsprint. If you use a photograph, make sure there is strong contrast in the photo so that it will reproduce reasonably well. You don't want to use a photo with a lot of very fine detail because the detail will be lost on the printed page. You will need to have the photograph "screened," which is a process that converts a photograph into a dot pattern that allows the newspaper compositors to reproduce your picture more clearly. Some newspapers use a sixty-five-line screen, which is very course. A paper with better printing quality might suggest an eighty-five-line screen. If your photo, when printed in the paper, looks a little "muddy," next time you might consider going to a coarser screen.

Another consideration is the use of color. You can buy "spot color," which will draw more attention to your ad by using an additional color in one part of the ad. For example, American Express might print the illustration of its charge card in green and its logo and a few choice phrases in blue, but the rest of the ad would be in black and white. Because color printing is more costly, you need to determine if the additional cost of the color brings in enough additional business to justify the use of color.

Newspaper Classified Ads

Classified advertising is an entirely different animal than display advertising. As with the Yellow Pages, classified advertising is one of the few forms of advertising where interested buyers actively seek out your advertising. So if you're selling some very specific items or services you may want to test out using the classifieds. Classified advertising is relatively inexpensive. You can buy a very small ad, and if your ad offers benefit to the buyer it can still make an impact. As with display advertising, you want to employ a benefit headline but a very brief one. And you want to include a call to action in which you ask the reader to call you or to visit you.

Many people that advertise in the classifieds waste space and therefore money by repeating the section heading in their ad. The newspaper's classified advertising people will place your ad in a appropriate category so potential buyers can easily find what they're looking for. When trying to sell a 1969 Mustang, you don't have to say "USED CAR FOR SALE" anywhere in the ad because the ad will appear in the used-cars-for-sale section. Instead, use a benefit headline like "CLEAN AND MEAN '69 MUSTANG."

National Newspapers and Magazines

You may want to consider advertising in a national publication that offers a regional or local edition of its publication. For example, the *Wall Street Journal* offers four regional editions: Northeast, Midwest, Western, and Southwest. It also has eighteen metropolitan editions that focus on such targets as New York/Philadelphia, Chicago/Milwaukee, Cleveland/Pittsburgh; Washington/Baltimore, and New England (Boston). If you think *Wall Street Journal* readers are prime customers for your product or service, it may be worth testing some ads in one of these special editions.

Time, Newsweek, and other national magazines mix nationwide ads with ads for regions. Thus the *Time* magazines distributed in Atlanta and Boston would both have ads for such national products as Pepsi and Ford cars, but the Atlanta *Time* might carry an ad for a southern supermarket chain and a southern brand of beer while the Boston *Time*V would include ads for New England products and services. If you want to target customers in a particular region, it might be a good idea to explore placing on ad in one of the regional editions of a nationally distributed magazine.

Keeping that in mind you may want to use zones or regions for testing and bracketing offers. Let's say your local paper offers six zones and your business pulls customers in three of those six. Out of the three zones, zone A, gives you twice the response of the other two, and zone B is 25 percent stronger than zone C, yet zone C still pulls enough customers to make it worth your while to advertise in it. You could have three different offers, one for each zone. The strongest zone could include the weakest offer while the weakest zone could contain the strongest offer.

Another service many papers offer is called a "split run." You advertise to the entire circulation but you can change your ad in the zones to see which ad works best. The newspaper will charge you for each split, but this form of testing helps you best understand what price points, headlines, or even specific items pull the strongest.

Tabloid Newspapers

In any given city there are many different tabloid papers that appeal to different customers. You'll probably find a business newspaper or journal; an entertainment newspaper; specialty papers for real estate, autos, and soon; a tabloid consisting of nothing but classified ads; and papers for the political, college, or minority communities. Each of these publications provides an opportunity to reach very specific groups of people.

The frequency of publication for tabloids may vary from daily to weekly, to biweekly, to monthly, to quarterly. A tabloid can be the same size as the daily newspaper or half that size.

Some tabloids are given away and others are mailed only to paid subscribers. The response from these publications can very greatly, so you want to test them before making a major commitment. Test a coupon if you can. If you doubt the publication's ability to reach your customers, run a very strong offer, for example, a full-service car wash for 50¢, a movie rental for 10¢, a Big Mac for 25¢, an oil change for $4.95, and so on. These are the kind of offers you would make in a major ad campaign. You're only using the ad to test the power of the publication to reach your potential customers. If you use these kinds of very strong offers and the redemption rate is low, you'll know that the publication is weak in terms of potential customers. On the other hand, if your coupon deal brings a rush of new customers, you may want to work that publication into your regular advertising program.

The big advantage of tabloids is that it costs you much less to plan an ad in a tabloid than in the daily newspaper. Moreover, you can target by specific interest or geography. Some tabloids will even do stories about you if you ask them to, or let you submit your own articles when you buy advertising from them.

The Yellow Pages

Yellow Pages ads are a must-buy for many types of businesses. When someone needs something, he or she often begins by looking in the Yellow Pages to find a solution to his or her problem. The key to buying ad space in the Yellow Pages is to buy as small an ad as you think you can get away with. Yellow Pages advertising is very expensive.

Again, use a strong headline. This is critical. Also make sure the copy offers strong benefits to the reader. The bigger the ad, the more it costs, but the better the placement your ad will receive.

Don't let your Yellow Pages sales rep talk you into something you don't really want. They are the best high-pressure salespeople you'll ever meet, and they use fear very effectively in their presentation. Be prepared. Your ad is too important to let the Yellow Pages people design it for you. Because of all the money you're likely to put into Yellow Pages advertising, pay a little more to have a professional design yours. If you have camera-ready art all set to use, the sales rep will not be able to push you into the next largest size. To complicate matters, they will try to sell you spot color or full color to enhance your ad. And to complicate matters even more there are new publications trying to compete with the Yellow Pages, so you'll be hearing from more than one sales representative.

Using Your Competitor's Ads

Keep your eyes open for competitors that fail. A private investigator in Akron, Ohio, was able to benefit when one of his competitors went out of business. That competitor had a Yellow Pages ad twice the size of his own. He found out that the defunct company had used an answering service and that the service owned the phone number. So while keeping his own phone number, he paid the answering service a nominal monthly fee to secure his former rival's number. As a result, his business doubled at hardly any cost to him.

If you want to use this idea, try contacting the phone company when a competitor goes out of business to buy the use of its phone number. Bob Kramer of Kramer's Sew & Vac in Cincinnati found an even better way to be a Streetfighter when one of his competitors went out of business. Normally when a business ceases to function, the phone company adds a "This number is no longer in service" message to its dead phone number. Bob Kramer contacted the former owner and paid him $100 to contact the phone company and request a message to announce a number change instead of a disconnect. The new number is Kramer's!

This is one of those ideas that may not work every time, but is certainly worth a shot. The worst that can happen is that your offer will be refused. But if it works, it can mean a big jump in your inbound calls.

Chapter Summary

Newspaper advertising can be effective yet very costly in most markets due to limited competition. Tabloids, shoppers, and speciality newspapers might be able to reach your potential customers for less money, but they need to be tested.

Yellow Pages advertising can also be effective because it is one of the few forms of advertising where potential customers proactivly seek out the advertisers.

Ad size, placement, the use of color or illustrations, and copy are elements that factor into the success of print advertising. Generally you want to by the smallest, least expensive ad you feel will do the job.

12

Radio Advertising

B roadcast advertising on TV, cable, or radio is usually too expensive to be used by a Streetfighter. However, with radio, generally the most cost-effective of the three if you have a limited budget, there are some tips that can help you to create inexpensive and very effective ads.

However, if you cut too many corners, the ad will be a waste of your money. Most stations will write and produce your commercial for free. But the resulting ad will sound like a bargain-basement product. Creating your commercial message for radio might warrant hiring a good writer. Commercials can range from the straightforward and factual to the crazy and humorous. Sometimes you can create an effective commercial using yourself as the talent, but the danger of this method is that the ad might sound amaturish. However you decide to approach you radio spot, make sure that the message is one that sells the benefit of what you do or sell to the listener.

To make your ad stand out, you may want to hire a good "voice talent" to do your "voiceover." Most local disk jockeys sound like local disk jockeys, so if you want your spot to stand out it, you should consider investing in an announcer with a unique voice.

Being the voice in your own radio commercials has some benefits. First, it will be unique. Second, it helps make you a local semi-celebrity, which is very useful when you meet your customers one on one. My advice is: If you can sell on the radio, do it. If you don't have an effective delivery, but still want to take part in your ads, hire a professional to "interview" you in the ad so you don't have to carry the whole message all by yourself. A good producer can be very helpful in creating effective "interview" spots.

Be very careful with humor. Some spots amuse the listeners but don't convince them to buy the product or service advertised. It's not your job to entertain the masses; your job is to get your benefit across and increase sales. If you can do that with humor, great. But if it takes a different approach, use the nonhumorous approach.

Buying Your Schedule

Choosing a Station

Don't waste your money by spreading your ads across too many stations. Radio is a frequency medium, more so than any other media. Your customers must hear your spot repeatedly before they'll even begin to remember it, let alone act on it. So, if the radio station you choose to advertise on is one that tends to keep its audience, you will need to run fewer spots than on a station where there is a lot of "button pushing" during the commercials.

The listeners' "loyalty factor" will show up in the ratings. Stations whose format is all-talk, easy listening, and classical music tend to hold their audiences. Stations with formats like "Top 40," oldies, and rock, have a more fickle audience. Country audiences can be very loyal to a country station, but if there is more than one country station in your market, you may find that many country fans are "channel surfing."

Flighting

Some advertisers save money by concentrating their spots into "flights." When their budget is limited, they'll run spots regularly for a period of time. Then they'll take a hiatus. Then they return again with strong spot concentration. This on-again, off-again strategy is called "flighting."

Cost per Listener

You don't choose the radio station for your ads solely on the basis of its ratings, format, or degree of audience loyalty. With radio there are two elements to the ratings you have to factor into your station analysis. The first is "Average Quarter Hour." This is the number of listeners who tune into that station in a given fifteen-minute period. The second element is called "Cume," which is the cumulative audience for that entire daypart. For example, Station WAAA may have an Average Quarter Hour listenership of ten thousand people and a Cume of fifty thousand. That means that the audience has turned over five times during that daypart.

Rival Station WBBB may have the same Average Quarter Hour of ten thousand listeners but a Cume of forty thousand. WBBB would have turned over its audience just four times. Given the same price for ads at both stations, and looking at the frequency of turnover, that is, how often the same person might hear your message over and over, Station WBBB is the better value for your ad dollar.

Cost per Thousand

The best way to compare radio stations to each other is by studying the CPM, or Cost per Thousand. You simply factor the audience size against the cost of the spot. Or better yet, you can have your sales rep do the math for you. Once you bring the cost per spot into the equation, the audience size, by itself, becomes a secondary factor. If Station WHAT has an audience size for a given daypart of ten thousand, and Station WOOP has an audience size of twenty thousand, you can't make your choice until you've factored the cost per spot on each of those stations. If the cost per spot on Station WHAT is $20, its CPM is $2.00: it will cost you $2 to reach every 1,000 listeners. And if station WOOP has a spot cost of $50, its CPM is $2.50. Station WHAT with its $2 CPM is the better value even though it has half the total audience size of its rival.

When using the CPM to choose a station, you should not ignore the total audience size. If the station is too small to have a significant impact for you, it will do you no good despite its attractive

CPM. For example, if you were to look at a third station, WIMP with an average-quarter-hour listenership of only five hundred and a spot cost of a mere 50¢ each, the CPM would be $1. That's half of WHAT and less than half of WOOP. Yet WIMP's total audience is so small that you probably would be wasting your money to try to reach it.

Not only do you use the CPM to tell which stations are best for your target audience but also which dayparts. Morning and afternoon drive times generally have the largest audiences and therefore cost the most. As a result, many stations price their midday and evening ads at a discount.

Getting More from Your Rep

You can stretch your ad budget by doing some street-smart negotiating. Set your budget up-front and negotiate for the number of spots. In addition, consider using a live announcer tag at the end of your commercials. This is usually the last five or six seconds during which the disk jockey comes on live and makes a special announcement such as, "That's tomorrow at Jeff's Gym, so don't miss it. Only twelve seats left. Call today."

A live-announcer tag has two advantages. First, you're more likely to get the last position in the commercial break. Most radio spots are played during commercial breaks made up of six, eight, or even more spots in a row. When the commercial breaks come on, listeners start hitting buttons on their car radios and changing stations. All things being equal, you're most likely to get the most listeners if you're the first or last commercial during a break.

By requiring the disk jockey to do a live-announcer tag, you're more likely to get that last position when he or she has to come on the air anyway to announce the weather, the traffic report, or the next song. During the break the disk jockey is very busy and would rather wait to do a tag because all the prerecorded spots begin one after another automatically.

Second, when you give the sales rep your five-second tag, try putting in about eight seconds' worth of information so that the disk jockey really has to rush to fit it all in. Also wait til the last minute to give the station your tag, and change it daily so the disk jockey can't prerecord it on your spot. Then write the tag so it's a tongue-twister. When the disk jockey gets the cue light to begin the tag, he or she will be in a rush to say, "That's this Tuesday, Thursday, and Saturday at twilight where its tantamount to tantalizing and teasing tons of tested tastebuds till timid titillation time and time again at Tim Tucker's Time-Out Grill." Try saying that ten times fast. Most disk jockeys will mess it up, then joke about it, and give it another try. There's also a good chance they'll mess up one of those words and accidently say something "bad" on the air. All this draws a great deal attention to your commercial because the jock is now adlibing and joking. It also gives you precious free air time. When you hear your spot get messed up, you call your rep and "complain," so that he or she promises to "make good" by running a free spot.

Flexibility

In addition to being cost-effective, radio also has much more scheduling flexibility than other advertising media. For example, some stations will let you air your spots according to prearranged favorable conditions. For example, if you sell pools or pool supplies people only think of your product when it's sunny. So you arrange for the station to play your spots only on sunny days. Or if you sell replacement windows and insulation, you wait till the forecast calls for subzero temperatures and snow. That's when your spots will make the most impact.

Remote Broadcast Packages

Radio is a terrific vehicle for your creative ideas. For instance, remote broadcasts can be a very effective approach to radio advertising because your spots are broadcast live from your location. The spot can be done over the phone or via a microwave transmission. Most stations offer a remote "package" that turns the remote advertising into an event. You're usually given a certain number of spots in various dayparts. You may also get some "mentions" during which the disk jockey briefly reminds the audience of the upcoming event. You also sometimes get so many "call-in" spots, live from your location, and they often include give aways from a major national sponsor, such as six-packs from a soft-drink supplier.

Broadcasting live, on location, creates a certain amount of excitement and often motivates people to stop by that "live" broadcasting site. Also, the spots are usually concentrated into a week before the event so impact can be made.

A very creative version of the remote broadcast was used by Tom Bramlett of Scuba Unlimited in San Francisco. He sells diving trips to his customers. On one such trip to Hawaii he set up a call-in remote. Once a day for a week, at a predetermined time, he would call the radio station and talk about the previous day's activities, both below and above the water. Since this was happening in "real time," it didn't promote that particular trip but it made a great impact in his stores for future trips. What made this promotion particularly good was that the morning disk jockey at this station was a certified diver and thereafter did other promotions with Bramlett over the years, including a remote broadcast from underwater at the bottom of a pool.

If you normally use radio, you might want to add this call-in approach to your business trip. For example, almost any businessperson attends annual conventions and trade shows, usually in resort cities. While on such a trip, you could use your radio spots to call in to the station and talk about new developments in your industry; such call-in spots can suggest to the listeners that you're on the leading edge of your industry.

Also, check around the radio station to see if any of the disk jockeys are enthusiasts of what you offer. If you sell motorcycles, find a disk jockey who rides motorcycles. If you sell art, find one who collects art. By working with this disk jockey and his or her station, you can create a very unique situation for yourself that makes great impact with the station's audience. Sometimes you can barter your products or services for the disk jockey's expertise about radio ads and he or she might give you a lot of free exposure on his or her show. Such exposure is a super supplement to your spot advertising.

On-Air Giveaways

Another flexible element of radio advertising is the ability to get your product or service used in the station's promotions. When you buy an ad schedule, you want to explore providing the station with gift certificates or products it can give away on the air to its listeners. Or they can be used as prizes during the station's contests. On-air tributes to your generosity in providing a product or service is great exposure for you and your product or service, and this exposure will have an additional impact on the audience that knows you through your regular spot schedule.

Testing and Tracking Radio Results

Broadcast advertising is often tough to track, but you want to figure out a way to get an indication of how well your spots are working. There are several ways to do this. One way is to ask the listener to mention your radio ad in return for something extra. Or you could offer "a radio coupon." All you have to do is tell listeners to make their own coupons by using the information you provide and then bring them in for the savings, value, or free gift you offer.

To test a new radio station in this manner to really determine if it has an audience that will respond to your ads, make your first offer superattractive. If the ad doesn't pull, you'll know that your message isn't reaching the people you want it to reach.

If you are in the automotive-service business, you can easily determine which stations your customers listen to by seeing what station the car radio is tuned to when it is brought in. Thus if you do oil changes and lubes, do muffler or brake work, or sell tires, and so on, have your personnel turn on the car radio and run through the preset buttons to determine the stations a customer listens to.

Weather Closings

No matter how small you are, when the weather is such that other businesses are calling in to radio stations to announce closings, you do the same. I know the owner of a small print shop who had a Streetfighter's savvy. When blizzards hit and his area's big companies closed down and announced those closings on the radio, he would call in to announce that all three shifts at the XXX Print Company should report for work. "All three shifts" happened to be him, his wife, and his two kids after school, but this ploy got his business free exposure.

Chapter Summary

Radio advertising can be an effective and flexible medium for those with modest budgets. You can select stations that target very specific demographic groups and you can usually negotitiate additional exposure. When negotiating, always set the budget up-front and stick with it. Then ask for additional spots or better placement.

To have more impact, concentrate your advertising on one or two stations because the more money you spend on any one station the more they're likely to give you a good price. Also, concentrate your ads in a few-day period or a particular daypart to ensure that listeners hear your commercial repeatedly. Radio remote broadcasts turn your advertising into an event, and on-air giveaways draw more attention to your products and services.

13

Outdoor Advertising

Billboard ads are very costly and sometimes hard to place. Many communities are putting tough restrictions on billboards and other kinds of advertising signs. With fewer billboards available, those that remain often sell for a premium.

The best way to use a billboard locally is as a directional, that is, as a sign to direct traffic to your location: "For Jim's Diner, turn left at the next exit." Keep your billboard simple, using perhaps six words in the headline and only three elements in the board. A board that is too busy and hard to read is going to be ignored: motorists don't have a lot of time to read a billboard. One of my favorite boards is for Red Roof Inns. The Red Roof name and logo appears with a two-word message, "Sleep Cheap!," that is simple, memorable, and effective.

Sometimes two noncompetitive advertisers can share the same billboard. This may work if the two advertisers are located near each other and can get across their message in half the space. The advantage of splitting a board with another business is that the cost to you is usually just a little more than half of what it would cost you for a full board.

There are two major types of boards: painted boards and paper postings. Painted boards are generally much larger and the message is painted directly on the panels. You can also use "appendages" on painted boards, extensions that go beyond the traditional perimeter of the board. While it will cost you more, such appendages do make a great impact when they are done right. Some of the most powerful ones are in Orlando, Florida, enroute from the airport to the major amusement areas.

Paper postings, or "30-Sheet" postings, are printed on paper and then pasted to the billboard. The cost of the printing for these paper postings goes up with the number of colors you use. Each paper posting is made up of many squares of printed paper that are hung by billboard workers much like a puzzle.

If you use a paper posting, it's a good idea to order some extra copies of the entire board. Then if you have a booth at a trade show or an event like the county fair, you can use the paper postings to make a powerful back drop for your booth.

It was once suggested to me by a billboard account executive that to get more exposure for the money, you might try running your billboard ad every other month for a year. When you rent a board for twelve consecutive months, you receive a small discount. However, by going with an ad every other month for a year, you pay for only six months. Do billboard companies immediately run out the first day your board expires and replace it with someone else's ad? Sometimes yes, and sometimes no. You're likely to find that you'll get the equivalent of 10–30 percent of free exposure by using this method. Your production costs will be little higher because you'll need to use more paper postings with this system, but it might be worth it. The system works even better when you change locations for your boards on the months you're up. I've had boards that stayed up for six months after I stopped paying for them.

The only other point of negotiation for billboard use is the specific location. The more people that drive by a location, the more valuable it is to the billboard owner. You need to compare that traffic count against the cost of the billboard to decide whether a board in a high-traffic area is worth the cost.

For this reason, it's always a good idea to drive by the locations you're considering and see if there is anything unusual in the area that might work for or against you. For example, one board might be in a high-traffic area, but if it was surrounded by competing billboards that board wouldn't be worth its premium price. In the winter the location may be fine, but come spring half the board could be covered by a tree that was barely noticeable only a few months earlier.

Is there road construction near your billboard site? How does this affect your message? If your billboard is near a two-lane road that funnels into one, there may be less traffic but each passing car will be spending a lot more time near your sign. In this case you may want to consider changing your message from a brief one to a longer one. You might also use the road construction to negotiate a better deal for you with the billboard company. Most billboard companies don't discount their boards. Yet if you can raise a legitimate concern, in this case, the reduced traffic count, you might get a concession. You may not receive a dollar discount, but you might get extra weeks for free or a better deal on your next rental. It's worth a shot.

By the same token, if you know road construction is planned or in the works, and that great deal of traffic will be rerouted, look at some billboard locations that will be the beneficiaries of the additional traffic. Since their traffic counts will based on the company's last survey of that location (held before the reroute), you might be able to rent a discount billboard that will give you the exposure of a premium billboard.

Alternatives

There are alternatives to billboards, such as junior boards (smaller boards) and signs on bus shelters, on benches, and on and in buses, taxis, and subways. Many people trying to build a customer base might consider these other forms of outdoor advertising as "hokey." However, in major metropolitan areas, transit advertising and other alternatives can be very effective. But consider the message and the marketplace carefully before investing in these advertising tools.

Some small businesses "rent" the side of their buildings for advertising. The advertising message is painted directly on the brick siding. One advantage of working directly with the small business owner to put up such a message is that you have more flexibility in your negotiations than you would with a billboard company, and sometimes you can get what you want with barter instead of cash.

You could put up small directional signs near your business to help people find you. One apartment complex did this by approaching all the businesses at the major intersections within a few blocks of the complex. The manager offered to provide free grass cutting in exchange for putting up a directional sign. Since he had his own groundskeepers, it cost him practically nothing to have his people take care of six small sites near the complex.

A billboard posting can be very effective when used as another form of directional, that is, when it is there to inform the potential buyer *what store* he or she can buy a certain item at. This works particularly well with goods and services that already have a big demand and awareness, or when the parent manufacturer is running a big mass-media campaign.

A local power equipment retailer used billboards in this way when their manufacturer, Toro, was launching a large national TV campaign at the beginning of their season. There was a great deal of exposure for the products, and the TV and magazine ads sold the benefit of that product line. With all of this exposure for the product, the local retailer's advertising was specifically geared to getting customers into his store to buy Toro products from him. The billboards used the simple headline "Your Toro Headquarters" and his company name and logo.

Exterior Signs

Communities are getting more and more restrictive with their rules about signs. But if you don't have a good sign in front of your store or office, you make it difficult for your customers to find you, plus you're loosing an opportunity to create exposure for your business to the traffic that goes by your location every day. This is particularly critical for those businesses that are paying a premium to locate on busy streets or intersections. You want to create as much exposure at that location as possible.

Here are a few ideas to help you perhaps "skirt" some of the restrictions some communities have imposed. Before doing any of these, however, you must make sure you fully understand the local covenants and laws.

According to Daniel R. Rubin, an attorney in Columbus, Ohio, who represents numerous businesses nationally, "Before creating any signs be sure to check your commercial space lease to ensure there are no restrictions in regards to the size or nature of the signs you're considering. Check and review local ordinances which will not only inform you as to actual restrictions but will also inform you as to the proper procedures to acquire a variance if necessary. Lastly, it is always wise and saves you time and money in the long run to consult with your attorney before proceeding with any sign program."

If you're not allowed to have a sign near the street, you could make sure to keep a van or truck painted with your company name, logo, and/or slogan, parked near the street. Your vehicles are an extension of your business, so you do want to have notable signs on them. One business owner was taunted by his competitor for being small. So on his single delivery vehicle he painted on the left side, "Delivery Vehicle #1." The right side said, "Delivery Vehicle #2." The back read, "Delivery Vehicle #3." And the front read, "Delivery Vehicle #4." Overnight this businessman had created a fleet.

Signs for the Times

Jerry Roth of G. M. Roth Construction, in Nashua, New Hampshire, changed his job-site signs from ordinary realtor-type signs to bold blue-and-white signs mounted on high-visibility, bright-blue sawhorses. He then redid his truck signs to match this new look. Thereafter his leads jumped nearly 20 percent and his sales increased nearly 24 percent. G. M. Roth converts one of every three sign leads to sales averaging $9,000, according to an article in *Remodeling*.[8]

That same article mentioned Marvin Wilson of Peoples Carpentry, in Ann Arbor, Michigan, who designed a four-sided sign with roof and gables that he uses on his largest projects. The base sign cost $200 to construct and is repainted to match each home being remodeled, at a cost of $75. What could better express his market niche: high-end, full-line remodeling with an emphasis on fine woodworking and craftsmanship?

For those of you in professions where signs on your car wouldn't be proper, you may want to take advantage of vanity license plates. Dr. Neil Baum, a urologist in New Orleans, has a plate that reads "THE WIZ." Sandra Gurvitz, a freelance writer for several publications, including *People magazine*, has the plate "WDSMTH." Here are some more examples:

Attorney: "I SUE4U."
Veterinarian: "DOG DOC" or "CAT DOC"
Psychologist: "IOK UOK"
Accountants: "I AUDIT," "TAX CUT," and "1040."
Quick oil change: "10 W 40" and "10 W 30"
Payroll service: "W TWO."
Stockbroker: "IBUY LO" or "ISEL HI."
Optometrist: "ZMXYSW" or "EYE DOC"
Butcher or Karate Instructor: "I CHOP"

A professional-speaker friend of mine has a plate that reads, "I SPEAK," and another has the plate "NSPIRE." Such plates are great attention getters and conversation starters at cocktail parties.

Competitive Attack Backfire

Sometimes a simple message combined with a powerful tactic can really make an impact. Consider the case of a major national fast-food restaurant in Virginia Beach, Virginia. For years it was the only fast-food restaurant on this resort peninsula. Then one of its major competitors opened a restaurant nextdoor. The competitor advertised its grand opening. On the day of the grand opening of this competitor, the veteran fast-food restaurant put this message on its marquee: "In honor of our new neighbors, we will be closed today." The new competitor was so overwhelmed with customers due to the untimely vacation day of the operation nextdoor that it offered slow service and ran out of food. The restaurant's customers were disappointed or angered, and many never returned. In six months the new competitor left the market.

Marquee Basics

Movable-type signs are powerful ways to communicate with existing and potential customers. Don't let this opportunity go to waste. Here are some guidelines for effective use of these signs:

1. Change your message weekly. Messages get stale very quickly and you don't want the traffic to get used to your message. Even if you want to offer the same information, change the wording enough to make it look like a change of message.
2. Change lightbulbs as needed. There's nothing more tacky than a sign with bulbs burned out. It's harder to read and makes you look bad.
3. Keep plenty of letters on hand. They can break easily, so make sure you have a good inventory of the letters, numbers, and symbols you use most. Using an "E" backwards for a "3" looks tacky. The letters are not that expensive. In an emergency you can play these games, but don't make it a habit. Ask yourself what a billboard would cost at your location per month, and you'll begin to see the value of doing your sign right.
4. Never display an empty sign. It gives the impression that you're closed.
5. "Selling" messages are generally better than "touchie-feelie" messages. If you want to wish the local high school basketball team good luck, give them a call on the phone. Sign space is valuable, and it shouldn't be taken for granted.
6. Stay away from cutsie or funny sayings if they don't sell your product or service. They might get people to notice your sign, but if they don't bring customers into your store, what good are they? Stick to basics and find another avenue to express your creative talents.
7. Keep messages simple and easy to read.
8. Monitor your sign daily. You may find that your letters have been rearranged by some creative wordsmith, and this could prove embarrassing.

Chapter Summary

Billboard advertising can be very costly because of limited availabilities due to increased sign restrictions in many communities. The two main types of billboards are painted, which are larger, and 30-Sheet paper postings, which are printed on paper. The best way for most local businesses on a limited budget to use billboards is as a directional to guide customers to the location.

Alternatives to billboards may work for you at a fraction of the cost. These include junior boards, transit advertising, and bus shelters. There also may be possibilities of renting the side of a building to paint your message for a reasonable investment.

Advertising on your automotive fleet also provides exposure in the marketplace, and vanity license plates get attention when they are creative. Marquees are also effective when the message is changed often and is used primarily for promoting your business.

14

Diaries of
Streetfighting Marketeers

When I teach the Streetfighter Marketing program to a variety of clients, one of the more difficult concepts to fully explain is "longevity." It seems that many businesses are looking for the "magic wand" or the "silver bullet" to magically increase their sales in ninety days or less. The truth is, that while you should have some improvement over the short term, the significant impact of Streetfighter strategies takes consistent effort over time.

One single promotion conducted by one single manager at a single location isn't a Streetfighter program. That promotion may bring in some new customers, but why stop there? The real benefit of the Streetfighter strategy comes from the accumulated results of *many* promotions, conducted over *time*, by a *number* of locations. Continuity makes the significant impact on your sales. A good Streetfighter manager or owner of one location should do thirty or forty promotions over the course of a given year. The first year the novice Streetfighter may do more because he or she is still learning the ropes, and there's some trial and error involved. After that first year, however, the experienced Streetfighter should have a really good idea of what will work in that community.

Out of the thirty or forty some promotions that the novice Streetfighter manager did in that first year there are perhaps twenty he or she may want to repeat the next year because of their success. Each year builds on the success of the previous year.

This chapter illustrates what a typical promotional period might look like. The illustrations are based on two different hypothetical businesses. Although the businesses themselves aren't real, the promotions I present are ones that have actually been done by real businesses. They illustrate how you can create momentum, by using a variety of promotions, of varying intensity, over a period of time.

Don't be concerned if you happen to have a different type of business than the ones I use for illustration. The program works if you own a hair salon or a service station, a travel agency or an optical service, a dry cleaners or an insurance agency. The actual promotions or their implementation may vary, but the idea is the same.

Diary of a Family Restaurant

JANUARY

Promotion #1: My first promotion is a certificate exchange. I want to work with another business whose customers are much like mine. I have a new menu featuring five new items approved by the American Heart Association. They have reduced salt, cholesterol, fat, and calories. I also realize that most people decide to do something about their diet and fitness right after New Year's Day. Diet centers and health clubs often have their busiest times in January so I decide to cross-promote with a health club located three miles away.

The health club has 2,500 members. I arrange to include in their monthly newsletter a certificate that gives them a special savings on any of the five "heart-healthy" items on my menu. The health club mails these certificates to their members as a value-added item.

Promotion #2: Things tend to slow down in January so I decide to spice things up a little in the middle of the month by having an employee-referral contest. My restaurant has fifty employees. Each one, if they choose to be in the contest, gets fifty cards that award a free desert with the purchase of an entree at the regular price. The employee signs and dates the card to make it valid, and it expires two weeks after the date of distribution.

Each employee must hand out the cards on his or her own time and cannot hand them out anywhere inside the property line of the restaurant, including the parking lot. I divide my employees into ten teams of five. The teams and the individuals with the most redemptions win prizes. I award both weekly prizes and grand prizes at the end of the one-month contest period. If employees need more cards, I will provide them. At least 2,500 cards are personally handed out to friends, relatives, and acquaintances of the employees.

Promotion #3: As January comes to a close I realize that Valentine's Day is just around the corner. I ask myself, "What stores within a ten-minute drive of our location do a big business for Valentine's Day?" Four come to mind immediately: florists, candy shops, jewelry stores, and card shops. Then I add maid services and women's clothing stores. So I do a two-week blitz to help me dominate the season and set up promotions with six different merchants, all within five miles of my location in honor of Valentine's Day. All six owners or managers of these different businesses are customers of mine, so I actually set up the promotions when they visit me.

I create a coupon booklet containing special Valentine's Day offers from each of the six merchants and I hand them out to my customers during the two weeks before Valentine's Day. The cover of the booklet also has an entry form for a contest whose prizes include a free dinner for two, a corsage and a boutonniere, a two-pound heart-shaped box of chocolates, a gold heart-shaped locket necklace, and one free house cleaning. People register to win at any of the participating seven merchants (including me). This contest is promoted internally at each business with fliers, table tents, handmade posters, and danglers. Some participants are going to mention the contest in their regular media advertising.

The neat thing about this promotion is that with seven different merchants handing out the booklets we all get tremendous distribution of our special offer. We agree to share the cost of printing.

FEBRUARY

Promotion #4: Certificates are now coming in pretty steadily for the Valentine's Day promotion and contest. To be valid, the entry form for that contest required the participant's name, home address, workplace address, and phone number. About three thousand people have entered the contest. I do two things. First, I make a scattergram. I put up a street map of the area on a bulletin board in the back room. Then I pull every tenth card from the contest and plot the card owner's home address on that map with a red pin and his or her work address with a blue pin. It takes a couple of employees about three hours to plot a total of five hundred pins (three hundred red and two hundred blue).

The map tells me when my new customers are most concentrated. It's no surprise that the concentration of pins increases closer to the restaurant *store*. By five miles out, the pins are few and far between. But I do notice one little spot about three miles to the north of my restaurant on a main street where the pins thin out more than usual. Why? Well, right in the middle of that bald spot lies a major competitor! Of course. So I need to do a major cross-promotion just on the other side of that competitor to encourage some of those people to consider driving past that restaurant to come to mine.

I see that there's a major department store a couple blocks north of my competitor. The manager of that store eats in my restaurant occasionally. A cross-promotion will distribute twenty thousand certificates to their customers for us in one week. My offer is a strong one since I have to get those people to bypass my competitor.

Promotion #5: I still have those three thousand names from the Valentine's Day contest, so it makes sense to do a targeted mailing. I had six prizes to give out to six happy winners, but why can't I issue 2,994 consolation prizes? February is usually still a little slow, so I offer one entree at half price with the purchase of another at the regular price. That's a fairly strong offer. A "BOGO" (Buy One, Get One Free) would be stronger, but I prefer not to discount that deeply unless I really have to.

Now I have to make sure that my mailing will be read. To do this I use a picture-postcard mailing. While I was in Las Vegas for a National Restaurant Association convention, I picked up three thousand picture postcards of Las Vegas and got a great price for buying in quantity. I print "Congratulations, You Won Second Place!" on the back of the postcards, and ask the customers to bring in the post card for their consolation offer. I mail out three hundred cards at the postcard rate of 19¢ to test the promotion. If the response is strong, I'll mail the rest by month's end.

MARCH

Promotion #6: The weather's starting to break a little and business is picking up, as it usually does about this time of year. Saint Patrick's Day is about two weeks away. That's an easy one. I'll have a big celebration on the seventeenth with green everything. I will promote it internally.

Promotion #7: We're all saddened to find out that Allison, the diabetic daughter of one of the waitresses, must have a kidney transplant. Her father is donating one of his, but the family desperately needs to raise money to pay for the operation. Family and friends, with the support of their church, have vowed to do whatever fundraising is necessary to pay for this life-saving operation.

I offer my restaurant for a major fundraiser. This one event will be my main promotional focus for the next four weeks. There's much to do. The key is to structure the promotion so that we can raise the money Alison's family needs, while still keeping my profits up. I decide to hold the fundraiser in four weeks, on a Wednesday. I normally gross about $1,000 on an average Wednesday at this time of year. On that day, for every dollar I take in beyond $1,000, half will go to the cause. Now it's up to Alison's family and their friends to make sure that every person within five miles comes to eat here on that day!

I'm amazed at what they do. They get flyers and posters printed up at the local quick printer, who donates them. The headline reads "Eat with us and save a life." They're really making me look good. They distributed fliers everywhere. They hang posters on every telephone pole, in every business window, and in public places. They arrange for free announcements on the radio and in the paper. The local bookstore is handing out fliers as bag stuffers, and has created a special display of books on living with diabetes and other related health titles. On the day of the event the bookstore will set up that same display in my lobby, and will donate 25 percent of all sales to the cause. I love it.

Allison's school is also taking part in the effort. All the school children are going door to door and to hand out fliers. The school band is going to play in our parking lot on the day of the fund raiser. And now a radio station is jumping on the bandwagon. Not only are they running public-service announcements about the fund raiser, but one of the disk jockeys is going to broadcast live from the restaurant for four hours during the event.

The local bank branch has placed an announcement about the event on its electronic marquee and near their ATM machine. And one of the major grocery stores is doing a bag stuffer for the fundraiser.

Obviously, I'm going to have one busy Wednesday. I make sure that all my employees will be working: no one complains. In fact, they all said they wouldn't miss this for anything. If I need more help, a few of them have some friends who would be happy to pitch in. I also have to make sure that I have plenty of supplies so I don't run out. My soft-drink vendor has just agreed to contribute an additional 25¢ to the cause for every soft drink purchased.

The event was a tremendous success. We raised close to $3,000 and the family is thrilled. It's great to see Allison in such good spirits. We got tremendous exposure, including some free TV and newspaper coverage of the event. From a business standpoint, I served hundreds of new customers who had never been to my place. That has a tangible value to me. Moreover, business runs higher than usual the following weeks. It pays to be community-oriented.

Promotion #8: I knew we were going to have many hundreds of people at Allison's fundraiser and I wanted to make sure that first-timers are motivated to visit us again. I use a bounce-back certificate. Each person who supported the fundraiser received this special certificate, good for $1 in savings on their next meal. The customer has two weeks to use it.

APRIL

Promotion #9: Easter is a week away. There is a church just down the street from my restaurant. I usually get a half-dozen or so families here after church, but many go to other restaurants. I really want to get all that Sunday business, so I'm using Easter to kick off a promotion. Pastor James eats with us about once a week. Last time he was here I sat down with him. As I picked up the check, I said I had an idea I wanted to run by him. It's common knowledge that the church is in need of a new roof and that the congregation is planning all kinds of fundraisers to pay for the new roof. I told Pastor James that I had an idea that might help him raise some money. I would provide his congregation with special certificates. Whenever a member of Pastor's James's church purchased a meal at my restaurant and gave a certificate to the waitress, I would set aside $1 as a donation to the roof fund. I would give the Pastor two kinds of certificates: the yellow certificates were good only for Sundays after church, and the green ones could be used any other time during the week.

It was up to the church to make sure everyone received certificates and then redeemed them. The pastor was so excited by my plan he told me he was going to mention it from the pulpit and try to get everyone to my restaurant after church for the next four weeks! Since next Sunday will be Easter, I'm expecting great attendance.

I think I'll try this promotion with a few other congregations in the area in upcoming months.

Promotion #10: For the first half of April I set up a basic cross-promotion with H & R Block. Tax specialists attract a lot of clients during the first two weeks in April, and I want to turn some of H & R Block's clients into my customers.

Promotion #11: One of the area's major employers has a big plant with about two thousand workers about five miles down the road. I thought it would be great if I could do something to attract that group to my restaurant. I approached the plant's director of personnel about providing the workers with a special VIP card that would give them a 10 percent discount on meals whenever they eat at my restaurant, but the personnel director was not interested. Actually, he was quite rude to me. So then I approached the president of the plant's union. He was up for reelection in a couple of months and he just loved my idea. He intends to send out my VIP card to his two thousand union members with the local's monthly newsletter.

Promotion #12: Area high schools are gearing up for prom time. I want some of that prom business. A couple of members of the marching band work for me part time and they told me that they were in desperate need of new band uniforms. They were planning all kinds of fundraisers and wanted to know if I had any ideas. I guess they heard about my reputation for helping community groups.

We all sat down together and over some diet soda came up with a couple of ideas. We decided to hold a prom fashion show at the restaurant. The high schoolers knew the owner of a dress shop who was dying to do this, and I had a friend in the tuxedo rental business who I thought would be interested. They would also contact the florist to ask if she would provide the models with corsages and a few arrangements to decorate the place. The band members would promote the event to fellow students and sell tickets, and I would provide appetizers. After the fashion show everyone could stay for dinner: I promised to donate 25 percent of the money spent on meals to the band-uniforms fund.

We planned to hold the fashion show late on a Saturday afternoon when things are pretty slow. I expect most of those who attend to stay for dinner when the show ends at 5:00. The 25 percent offer will only be good for meals ordered before 7:00, so the fashion-show crowd won't interfere with my Saturday-night crowd. I will also offer a coupon booklet with special discounts from the other merchant participants plus a couple of "bounce-back" offers customers can use on their next visit to my restaurant.

MAY

Promotion #13: To take advantage of Mother's Day, I decide to do a few cross-promotions. I want to do three with three different businesses that do big business near Mother's Day: the Hallmark Gold Crown Shop Florist (who worked on the prom show with us), and a Fanny Mae candy store about a mile away. It's a standard cross-promotion: for every purchase made at any one of those three places, the customer will receive a coupon for a savings at my restaurant when they bring their mom in. Also every mother who comes to my restaurant on Mother's Day will receive a pink carnation, compliments of my florist.

Promotion #14: I want to promote take-out meals on the weekends since I'm almost at capacity in my dining area. I figure a simple cross-promotion with a major video rental store in my area should help. If people are renting videos, they are probably planning to stay at home and might be in the market for a tasty meal to go.

Promotion #15: Continuing my quest for more dinner-to-go business, I decide I could pick up some business during the week if I target two-career couples with children. Busy working moms often don't have time to fix dinner. The perfect cross-promotion partners to help me with this project would be daycare centers, and there are two in my area.

Also, when things are a little slow in the afternoon, I visit nearby office buildings, introduce myself to everyone who works in them, and distribute carryout menus and my business cards.

JUNE

Promotion #16: School ends in a week. I always provide a free dessert for an "A" on a report card. It's an old idea that I've used for years, but it really works. Some bright children come in with enough "A's" to provide desserts for their entire family. The school promotes my deal with a single announcement. But the deal doesn't really need much promotion since all the children know I make the offer every year. Also, if a student doesn't get an "A," but can show significant improvement, for example, like from a "D" to a "B," I give them a free desert too. Actually, they're the ones who really appreciate the promotion.

Promotion #17: Father's Day. My Ugly Tie Contest is another annual promotion that always works for me. On Father's Day children submit their father's ugliest tie for judgment. I hang all the tie entries on one wall. The fashion editor of the local newspaper, the owner of a well-known men's store, and a local image consultant form the panel that judges the ties. The five ugliest ties win, and their owners are awarded a free dinner for two. I get some great coverage from the paper and TV, plus I always fill my restaurant for days before and after the contest with people curious to see the ugly tie display. The men's store hands out certificate for savings at the store and the image consultant passes out brochures. The whole event is lots of fun, and profitable too.

Six More Months Left in the Year

This series of promotions illustrates what a typical first six months of the year would be like for a single restaurant. But, as I mentioned earlier, I could have just as easily offered six months in the life of a gas station, a clothing store, a real estate agency, a lawn and garden service, or any other kind of business. Obviously, the actual structure of the promotions would change to fit the product or service being sold, yet the basic concept of networking within a three- to five-mile radius doesn't change.

There are many types of promotions other than those mentioned in this six-month restaurant diary. Some are more elaborate and some are ridiculously simple. Notice that the owner in my example conducted seventeen promotions in six months. Actually there were more like twenty-two because some of his cross-promotions involved two or three different partners. Most of these promotions were simple and took little time. He always had something going on. He discovered opportunities or problems and created a promotion to improve the situation. Not all worked equally well, but over the six months he got very strong results. He's an integral part of his neighborhood. People want to do business with him.

Imagine the impact on your chain of three hundred fast-food outlets if even half your managers carried out promotions as often and as skillfully as the restaurant owner I have just described!

Diary of a Bookstore

Let me offer another example to give you a deeper appreciation of what can be accomplished by using Streetfighter promotional techniques. In the next promotional diary we'll look at a six-month effort for a bookstore. Promoting a bookstore and a restaurant may seem very different from each other, but you'll see that there are many similarities in the promotional techniques.

The big difference between these two retailers is that the bookseller has a narrower, more specialized customer base than a restaurant owner does. But what may seem to be a disadvantage is actually an advantage. The bookseller can look at each department within the bookstore as its own unique opportunity to do promotions to mystery readers, art lovers, gardeners, students, and so.

JANUARY

Overview: I usually average about two to four author book signings per month. My customers really love it when I provide them with an opportunity to meet authors and to buy autographed copies of their books. Still, I need to do other types of promotions to generate more business.

Promotion #1: In January many people make their New Year's resolutions. Books that deal with behavior modification might be of particular interest to the resolution makers during the first part of the month. I create a display of books that deal with healthy diet, exercise, weight loss, breaking the smoking habit, and the like.

To create more interest I approach a local hospital that's been very aggressive in its community outreach program and is looking for new ways to gain more exposure. I suggest we set up a weekend (Friday, Saturday, and Sunday) during which the hospital will conduct free hypertension screenings at my bookstore. We both agree to promote it. I'll mail an announcement to my customers and use a bag-stuffer flier. The hospital agrees to mail an announcement to its patient list; will include a similar announcement in all internal cooorespondance to staff, supporters, and vendors; will add a one-line message on its bills; and will set up posters in key areas of the hospital. The hospital PR department also intends to send out a press release to the news media a few days before the hypertension screening.

Promotions #2 & #3: The New Year's period often prompts people to try to learn new skills. I seem to sell a lot of computer books in January. To increase sales of computer books, I contact a company that trains people to operate popular computer programs. I invite them to do a couple of beginning-level lectures on two programs that I know my customers are interested in, the newest versions of WordPerfect and Windows.

They agree to bring their own computer, including an adapter to project their presentation on a big screen. They'll provide a three-page handout with information about the basics of each program, and of course information about their training courses. I'll create a special display of computer books near the presentations, and offer a discount on any computer books bought by customers who attend. I will also offer a "value-package" of books sold with a Word-Perfect miniflip chart of codes, capabilities, and a new template.

I promote the computer lectures in my monthly calendar, on bag stuffers, and with internal posters. I also send invitations to three hundred small businesses in my area. I was lucky enough to find a Radio Shack that was willing to pass out my fliers to their customers if I would provide my participants with a flier about their upcoming computer sale. I made a similar deal with a big business supply company that passed out my fliers in each of its orders in return for my promise to pass out its fliers during the lectures.

FEBRUARY

Promotion #4: I see in the current *TV Guide* that Fabio, the heart-throb male hunk who appears on the covers of romance magazines, is going to be a guest on "Live with Regis & Kathy Lee." Because of my limited budget, I can't afford regular TV ads. But a few ads promoting my store as the best place to buy romance novels should make an impact on the audience tuned in to see Fabio. I call the TV station to find out what it would cost to buy some fixed position spots on this show. Fortunately, the spots only cost fifty dollars each, and there is also one 10-second spot available at the station break that only costs twenty-five dollars. I buy two 30-second spots and a 10-second spot at the station break. My total cost is $125. The station ad people agree to put my commercial together with a voiceover and some slides and charge me twenty-five dollars to make the slides.

Promtion #5: Our local orchestra is looking for ways to raise funds, and I think I can help. I have dozens of coffee-table books in the performing arts category: big expensive books on such composers as Bach, Mozart, Beethoven, and Schubert, lavishly illustrated opera books, and other music-related titles including ballet and jazz books. Many of these books have been taking up shelf space and gathering dust for months. I would love to get rid of them, and don't mind sacrificing profit so long as I don't end up with a loss.

I propose a deal. If the orchestra will distribute my flyer listing a special sale of performing arts books to their patrons, and their patrons bring that flier to my sale, I will donate 50 percent of the price of any performing arts books they buy to the orchestra. If this promotion is successful, I will attract new customers, get rid of a number of slow-selling books, and free up valuable shelf space. Moreover, my proposal has made me a hero to the symphony, which has promised to run a free ad for my store in its programs for the upcoming season.

MARCH

Promotion #6: My nextdoor neighbor is a kindergarten teacher at the local elementary school. She is a big fan of the whole language program, which is literature-based. She told me that mail order companies promote the buying of books by kids by offering their teachers free children's books based on the size of the order. We brainstorm about how I can go after the children's business while providing something extra to their teachers. I have no problem coming up with a great list of children's titles that I can sell at competitive prices. We generate three other advantages I can offer. First, teachers who use my store instead of mail order will be awarded bonus points they can use to buy any book in my store: they won't have to limit their bonus to children's books. Second, I can fill everyone's orders twice as fast as the mail order house. And third, I can offer my store as a site for class field trips.

To promote the program, I decide to have my resident children's literature expert give a brief presentation about it at the next PTA meeting. At that time I will also donate a few choice children's titles to the school library and pass out information to interested parents and teachers.

Promotion #7: While I'm at the PTA meeting I will also give all the teachers and parents special VIP cards good for a discount at my store. The PTA has already agreed to distribute about 1,000 of these cards in the community for me.

Promotion #8: There's a nice family-style restaurant down the street from my store. I have lunch there at least once a week and the restaurant owner is a regular customer of mine. He's doing a fund-raiser for one of his staffs children, a diabetic, who needs a kidney transplant. I agree to stuff his fliers at my store and to create a special window display of books about diabetes and other health problems. On the day of the event I'll set up a health books display in his lobby. I will sell the books at regular retail price, but I will donate 25 percent of my gross sales receipts to the fund for the diabetic child.

Promotion #9: Its late March, tax season. I've got some very popular tax titles I want to promote. I put a three-person panel together to speak at my store to generate some interest. The panel includes a CPA (a junior partner from a major firm), the financial editor of the local paper, and a CFP (Certified Financial Planner) from one of the major brokerage houses. The CPA firm agrees to mail invitations to all of its clients and vendors. The CFP agrees to do the same, plus to laser-print an announcement on all client statements in the area for one month. The brokerage house is also going to pay for one ad in a local weekly business journal. The ad will focus on its CFP, but that's okay with me as long as it publicizes my event. The financial editor will do a story about the event and see that the announcement appears in the "Seminars" heading of the "Around Town" section in the Friday edition.

As a last-minute thought I call the IRS to see if they would also like to be represented on the panel. They tell me they would be happy to send someone, and that he or she will bring along a supply of tax forms. Their PR person will send press releases to all the broadcast media as well for us. Should be an interesting night.

APRIL

Promotion #10: I call this my "James Michner Promotion." I pick six of his books with titles that are very popular vacation destinations: *Hawaii, Caribbean, Mexico, Alaska, The Source* (Israel and Egypt), and *Space* (Kennedy Space Center in Florida). I then approach a large travel agency and provide it with six different promotional pieces featuring one of Michner's books, travel guides (like the Fodor's Series), and other titles relating to that location. I also create a generic travel flier for locations other than the six Michner-related destinations. The travel agency inserts my flier, which offers a special deal on these featured books, in all their ticket jackets. This will be an ongoing promotion for the year, but if the agency informs me about other popular destinations I can come up with similar promotions for them.

Promotion #11: The Great Book Trade-In Promotion. My next promotion is a low-liability, community-involvement program. The local literacy council is having an event to encourage people to donate old books that it can them provide to its literacy clients. To help, I run a promotion for a two-week period. Customers can bring in any old book—as long as its in good condition—and receive a token good for a special discount on the purchase of a new book. All the old books will be donated to the literacy council. The council does all the external promotion for me, including publicity and a mailing (which it can do at the nonprofit rate). I do the normal internal promotions—bag stuffers, posters, and so on—and note the event in my monthly calendar mailer.

MAY

Promotion #12: The After-Hours Sale. Once a year I have a special, by-invitation-only sale for my preferred customers. I hold it on a Sunday evening from 7:00 P.M. to 11:00 P.M. when the store is normally closed. Invitations are hand-addressed and look more like wedding invitations than junk mail. The invitations encourage the recipient to bring a friend. During the sale, besides, offering special prices on books, I give away books as door prizes. I get local authors to attend and sign books. I serve wine and hors d'oeuvres provided by a local restaurant in exchange for exposure. This year I will also have a string quartet performance, provided at a discount by the local symphony because of my symphony promotion back in February.

Promotion #13: The weather is getting warmer and people are starting to think about outside activities. I have many gardening books. I approach a large nursery in my area and suggest we do displays for each other. They have their landscape artist do a window design for my store that features plants and garden tools. In return, I will feature a card in the window that contains their logo and address. We agree to leave it up for ten days, including two weekends. My other window display will feature gardening books and related titles. I set up a book display near their register. We each bag stuff advertising for each other during the ten-day mutual promotion. Their flyer is stapled to a packet of seeds imprinted with their name.

JUNE

Promotion #14: A large corporation will be holding its annual meeting in our city. Over two thousand of its dealers and employees will come from all over North America for this conference. As a member of our local Visitors and Convention Bureau, I get a copy of the meeting program. I find out that two professional speakers will be featured. The first is Dr. Michael LeBouef, author of *Fast Forward: How to Win Customers and Keep Them for Life, GMP: The Greatest Management Principle, Working Smart*, and other business titles. The second is Susan RoAne, author of *How to Work a Room* and *Secrets of Savvy Networking*. I call the corporation's public relations office and suggest that it might be a good idea if the featured speakers' books were made available for sale after their talks, and I offer to sell them myself at a special price for conference attendees. The public relations people like this idea, but tell me they need to clear it with Le Bouef and RoAne.

LeBouef and RoAne love the idea. They also agree to stop by my store before they leave town to meet me and do a stock signing of their books.

I alert local business reporters that two celebrated business writers will be in town for the convention and that they'll also be making a brief appearance at my store. No doubt, some of these reporters will appreciate the tip, and if they eventually do stories on LeBouef and RoAne, they'll mention that autographed copies of their books are available at my store.

End of Diaries

It's easy to see that these two very different types of businesses both promote to their neighborhoods without spending a lot of money. When they do spend money on advertising they place it where it is most likely to bring in customers and they get it for a reasonable price.

One last point: even though they're very different types of businesses, the restaurant and the bookstore did similar promotions. However, each promotion was adapted to a specific opportunity. The restaurant did a fashion show. Could the bookstore have done the same? Yes. The bookstore owner would have done it a little differently, for example, by tieing a fashion show to a certain line of titles, but it certainly could be done.

Did you notice that there were a couple of promotions in which the restaurant owner and the bookseller interacted? The restaurant had a display of books for one of its events. The bookstore served hors d'oeuvres provided by the restaurant. Both businesses are in the same neighborhood and both are using similar ideas to accomplish different goals.

If the diaries had lasted for twelve months, you would have seen a few more types of promotions and special events. The second half of the year has different holidays and offers different opportunities. I could create a diary for a hundred different types of businesses, but if I did, this book would be the size of an encyclopedia. I have given you enough examples to teach you the main concepts. Now all you have to do is adapt my ideas and make them work for you.

15

Putting Your Streetfighter Marketing Plan Together

This chapter assumes that you are a multiunit operator (single-unit operators will not need to read this chapter). Once you have an idea about the different promotional techniques you can use in one location, your next step is to put an action plan together that allows you to fully develop and then put into action a program for all your other locations. For illustrative purposes, I will assume that you are a multiple-unit operator with two hundred locations. You have deep penetration in some markets and shallow penetration in others.

In this chapter you will learn a process to increase your level of success in getting a Streetfighter program implemented and maintained by a significant number of your locations.

The steps you use are:

1. Do initial research
2. Choose developmental markets
3. Customize your program
4. Roll out your program
5. Maintain your program

Do Initial Research

In this phase of the program you search for ideas you can use in your program. This book is a great first step. Once you're done with this book you need to adapt the ideas in it to make them work for your business. Then review other books and tapes on this subject. I've listed some of my favorites in the Resource Guide at the end of this book.

Reviewing the books and tapes will expose you to the variety of techniques you can use to promote a business on the local level. Once you know what to look for, study your own stores and their managers to find out what successful things they're already doing.

Also keep you eyes open for successful local promotions done by your competition or perhaps even promotions done by totally unrelated businesses that might have some application for your business. Read your trade journals and attend your trade shows and conventions. You may meet some colleagues who are in your industry but not in your marketplace, and who have great ideas. Also look to your suppliers and vendors. They may have some programs or ideas that can be useful to you.

Another way to uncover some of the promotions that have been done in your area is to do a computer search at the local library. You can search using the key words "marketing" and "neighborhood" or "local." The computer will locate articles that address those two topics. The computer will list the title of the article, its author, the name of the publication in which it appeared, when it was published, and the page numbers. Sometimes the computer will provide brief one-paragraph summaries that will give you an idea of an article's content. The summary can help you decide whether to look up the entire article to get all the details.

You can hire an intern from your local college or university to conduct this search for you. A marketing or journalism major is perfect because they often are looking for practical experience to present in a resume. You can usually pay them minimum wage, which they don't mind because they can often get college credit for the effort. We use marketing interns every semester and have found them to be good workers and eager learners.

Another way to get current information about promotions is to use a news-clipping service. This kind of service charges you a monthly fee plus a small charge for each article it provides you. The service's readers scan just about every daily newspaper and all the national magazines, as well as many trade journals, and create a databank of articles arranged into hundreds or thousands of categories. You choose the categories you want, and the service sends you everything that falls under those categories. You may want to exclude your own trade journals so you don't get charged for articles you have already read. You can make the criteria as broad or specific as you like.

Both the clipping service and the library computer search will turn up many articles, but only a small fraction of them will be useful to you. Even so, it's important to be as current as possible to stay one step ahead of your competitors. Once you've gathered up all the ideas you think can help your business, you're ready for the next phase.

Choose Developmental Markets

Before you put these ideas before your managers, you need to fully develop them. The more developed and proven they are, the greater your chances of success when you roll the program out to all your locations.

When we develop a program, we start with two or three "developmental markets." Ideally these markets have a concentration of cooperative, aggressive, motivated, and bright managers. You use only a small percentage of your total number of stores to participate in this developmental phase, yet you want enough participants to generate a variety of success stories.

Not all stores in a developmental market have to participate in this phase of the program. We usually work them in multiples of four or five stores because that's how many managers typically can be trained one-on-one at their own locations in a day. In a business with a couple of hundred locations or more you might want to start with twenty-five participants, from two or three different markets. Regardless of the size of your organization, the maximum number of participants in the developmental phase usually should not exceed fifty, and all should be located in no more than four or five markets. For smaller companies, the minimum number of participants is five.

You want to group your participants to reduce travel time and repetition during the training phase. From a logistical standpoint, you want to keep them in multiples of four or five within driving distance of a central location.

At the same time you do want to tap into several different marketplaces during your development phase, if possible. So, for a company that will use a total of ten participants, you're better off arranging two participating markets, each having four or five managers. This will give you broader exposure and experiences during this developmental phase. You must balance the benefit of this approach with the reduced costs associated with training ten participants in a single market.

Your choice of participants is very important to the success of the program. The developmental phase is very challenging because you'll be converting mostly generic ideas into promotions geared specifically for your business. Training and execution is therefore more difficult during the developmental phase than in the roll-out phase. For that reason, we don't refer to this as a test market. You're actually stacking the deck in your favor, so to speak. Pick managers who are most likely to use the ideas and make them work.

Also, in choosing your participants, you might want to have a few extras on hand. Often when you get the program going, you discover that some participants just won't make the effort you expected. Thus, to have a developmental group of twenty-five, begin with twenty seven or twenty eight. After the first month, or the second at the most, you'll know the three or four managers that are wasting your time and you should then drop them from the program. That leaves a good core group large enough to do what you need to do.

Customize Your Program

For the first six months to a year, you will put the bulk of your efforts into customizing your program. Customizing involves the following steps:

1. Create a custom ad slick packet
2. Write kick-off workshop outline and create audio-visual materials
3. Write and produce workshop workbook
4. Conduct full-day kick-off workshop with participants
5. On-site, one-on-one training (first week only)

6. Weekly telephone training and consultation
7. Weekly reminder and reinforcement memos
8. Monthly half-day group training sessions
9. Monthly progress summary report

Ad Slick Packet

While the markets and managers are being selected you can prepare the training and promotional materials. One important tool is the ad slick packet. A retail or service business will probably use a variety of different cross-promotions, community-involvement promotions, and internal promotions, many of which will require various types of certificates or printed pieces. To make it easy for your developmental group to use the ideas, prepare camera-ready shells that allow them to go to their local quick printer, drop in their address, phone, and whatever, and quickly have in hand the material they need. This does two things. First, it speeds up the process since the managers don't have to design and lay out their own promotional pieces. Second, you retain a certain amount of control of the promotions. The offers you suggest have been thought out. Each piece has all the necessary legal disclaimers and makes proper use of the logo. You ensure that the theme or slogan you use in your regular advertising is carried through these pieces.

Preparing the offers yourself will save you from the kind of headaches the owner of a large pizza chain had when one of his managers offered a value card that allowed 25 percent off the entire bill, all the time. No limitations. No expiration date. No disclaimers. People were passing these things along in their wills.

An ad slick packet contains generic camera-ready artwork for creating the different types of promotional pieces that will be used a business. The manager or owner only needs to have the printer insert their address and a phone to customize it. A typical ad slick within the packet is an 8 1/2" x 11" sheet of gloss paper stock printed with black ink. A typical adslick packet would contain the following sheets:

2-up: Cross promotion
3-up: Cross promotion

FIGURE 15-1 Example of a sheet from an ad slick campaign—a buck front, 6-up version.

4-up: Cross promotion
3-up: Value card
1-up: 12-in-1
6-up: Bucks (front)
6-up: Bucks (back)
1-up: Buck flier
4-up: Employee contest

If there are different offers on any one of the pieces all the variations would also be included.

Workbook

The participants at the workshop use their workbook throughout the program. It contains many different exercises that require the participant to write specific adaptations of techniques for his or her store.

For example, one exercise may require the manager to write down the names of ten merchants in her neighborhood who are already customers and would make good cross-promotion partners. After completing many similar exercises involving value cards, 12-in-1's, community involvement, employee and customer contests, and so on, the manager will have identified hundreds of opportunities specifically for her location. When these opportunities are prioritized with deadlines, the manager will have a complete plan of attack.

The workbook also contains all the reference information needed, along with samples of promotional pieces. This workbook, like the workshop itself, will be evolving a great deal in the first six to twelve months of the program. You can produce the workbook quickly and inexpensively using good word-processing software. Since the workbook will be updated regularly, print them in short runs. If you choose to use a three-ring binder for the workbook, you can incorporate the ad slick pack into it too.

Initial Kick-Off Workshop

With all the preparations done, the next step is to fine-tune the full-day interactive workshop that will train the participating managers in the program. It should offer more than lectures, overheads, and writing in the workbook. It should include a great emphasis on role-playing and practice. In the workshop you'll cover all the promotional ideas that make sense for your business. In a restaurant chain, for example, the main sections would include cross-promotions, community involvement, and internal marketing. If appropriate, you could include a module on the mass media like radio, TV, outdoor, and print advertising. If this particular operation is looking to do a lot of banquets and catering, you would also include sections on selling and telephone marketing.

The presenter should have a detailed outline from which to work, along with a full set of overheads and possibly video clips. This could be a sample of TV coverage that someone got as part of a community involvement program. By combining audio-visual aides (AV) with a strong outline and a detailed workbook, you will have a very powerful presentation.

On-Site, One-On-One Training

After the full-day workshop you might go out into the field with each participant. In the field, your goal is to set up the first promotion so the participating managers can see just how to do it. Then it's the participant's turn to play the lead while you provide the support. Once they've set up their first promotion, even if you had to hold their hands while they did it, you'll discover that you'll get a lot more participation from the managers.

Weekly Telephone Training

Next you do weekly telephone training and consultations. At a predetermined time, you get together with the manager over the phone and review his or her activities for the previous week. You address any problems he or she may have had and go over techniques that may help in the future. Then the manager sets goals for the next week. These goals are agreed to by the manager and not just handed down by you. You shoot for one promotion a week at this stage.

Weekly Reinforcement Memos

After the weekly telephone training session you write a brief memo about the conversation. This memo is in part a reminder of the goals you discussed and in part a motivational tool. After you've spoken together on the phone, you send the manager a written reminder to reinforce what you planned together. This enables you to have a minimum of two contacts with this manager every week. The ideal time to send your memo to the manager would be the next day. Pizza Hut, Inc., in Ohio, for example, used a wire service to get its memos out quickly to its twenty-eight participants during their developmental program.

One thing that contributes to the success of the program is that you never go beyond three or four days without some kind of contact with a manager. If there's a problem and he or she isn't able to get the program done, you want to know about this problem as soon as possible. With this constant pressure, the manager knows he or she is accountable.

Copies of the written memos are sent to the manager's immediate supervisor and up the chain of command. This helps you to show everyone what is going on in the program. At the end of the month you do a summary report of the memos, sharing the highlights.

Monthly Group Training

Once a month you bring everyone together for a half-day group training session. Again, you review the activities for the past four weeks and focus on everyone's success stories. In the remainder of the session you go over more advanced techniques, troubleshoot, and set goals for the next month. This session allows you to praise those who are doing a good job.

This process should go on for a minimum of six months, and ideally for twelve months, because each month, season, and holiday that the managers have to develop their promotions adds more depth to the developmental program before the rollout phase.

Customize Your Promotions

At the end of this development phase you not only have numerous customized promotions but you have several prototype markets in place. You're now ready to move to phase two: customizing the program before roll-out. You first rewrite the seminar outline, workbook, and presentation materials to incorporate all the specific examples, stories, and statistics created from the developmental markets.

An effective training element in the rewritten workshop and workbook is the extensive use of actual promotions successfully implemented by the developmental market participants. You'll know the story of how the promotion was set up, the number of pieces distributed and redeemed, the increases in sales and customer counts. Use a combination of quantitative and anecdotal evidence to prove to future participants that your program works. Make the developmental participants the heroes of your program. You should also make use of some big failures to illustrate what not to do. Not every promotion will be a success, so make sure your participants have realistic expectations.

Reproduce successful cross-promotion pieces in the updated workbook. For additional impact, have your participating managers run extra copies of each piece, a practice that adds very little to their printing costs. You can use these pieces to create a sample packet, is an envelope containing several dozen actual printed pieces used for the various promotions that you'll discuss in your workshop.

Also during the rewrite stage you might want to add various contingency promotions for such things as grand openings, remodels, change of local manager, competitive intrusion, competitive exit, access obstructions like road work or sewers, bad press, and so on. During the developmental phase you'll probably have an opportunity to deal with many challenging situations that can help other managers in your company.

Something to keep in mind at this point is that even though you're customizing the program prior to the rollout, it won't reach its final form at rollout. This is a dynamic program that is constantly changing, so the workbook and other workshop materials need to keep pace with program changes. The presentation and workbook should be updated regularly. You should also employ a newsletter or other communication device to inform managers of new developments, new twists, possible pitfalls, and so on. After one year you'll have a very powerful and useful program. After five years, you'll have one that's much better, more profitable, and more practical. The program just keeps building on its successes.

Roll Out Your Program

You now have your custom workshop updated with a new outline, workbook, overheads, samples, video clips, anecdotes and success stories, statistics, testimonials, and so on, and a revised ad slick packet based on the previous year's experiences.

With the new workshop you're ready to begin the roll-out process. You can roll the program out as quickly as you want to, but you might find that it works better if you do it gradually and in stages. If you own a national company and have three prototype markets in place, you might do no more than ten markets for three months as your next step. Then bring on new markets in at ninety-day intervals. You will find that once you've worked all the bugs out of the program the process goes much faster in the second phase then in the initial development phase. Of course, using ten markets in the first phase of the rollout is only a suggestion. If you own a very large company you may want to do more, but still consider phasing in the program in waves.

Meanwhile, you want to work some reinforcement elements into your program. A newsletter devoted specifically to Streetfighting ideas works great. The newsletter would recognize those managers who are doing good promotions and it should also share with the rest of the locations those successful ideas that are working. The newsletter should be distributed at least once a quarter, and preferably once a month when you have enough activity to support it. If your company already has a newsletter, add a Streetfighting column.

To keep the managers excited and motivated, you should send congratulatory notes to those managers who are doing exceptional work. Even a short handwritten note from the company boss gives a big boost to a manager's ego. Awards specifically for Streetfighting should be given out at companywide meetings or at the annual convention, alongside other types of recognition. In order for your Streetfighter program to be successful in the long term, it has to become an critical part of the company's culture with support and recognition from the top down.

If your organization has assistant-manager positions at its outlets, and if that position is used to groom managers of the future, the assistant managers as well as the managers should participate in the program. Also, Streetfighting should become part of the training program that any new management trainee undergoes. You may also want to review the profile you use when recruiting a manager so that a favorable attitude toward Streetfighting Marketing is a must for acceptance.

A good trainers program must also be developed. When managers in a given marketplace are trained and encouraged to do Streetfighting tactics, their area supervisors, district managers, and regional vice-presidents will need to understand what Streetfighting is all about. They not only need to be able to do it themselves, but they also need to be able to supervise and advise others who are following the program. If there is one weak link in the chain of command, the program could break down.

Consider an organization with one thousand stores throughout the United States. They are located in fifty different markets, with perhaps five to fifty stores in a given market depending on the market's size. For every ten stores there is one area supervisor, one hundred area supervisors in all. These one hundred area supervisors answer to a district manager, of which there are ten. The ten district managers then answer to the vice-president. If one area supervisor is not behind the program, it contaminates ten stores. If a district manager is aloof, it affects ten area supervisors and one hundred stores. It's critical to get support from the top down if you want this program to be done effectively by your one thousand locations.

Is it realistic to expect all one thousand stores to jump on the bandwagon? No. You'll probably find that your top two or three hundred stores will really go to town. And you'll probably also find that the bottom 20 percent just try to get by; they would do nothing if they could get away it with it. There will be varying degrees of success in the middle. For this reason, during the roll-out phase, I advise concentrating your efforts on your top 20 percent of stores and managers.

This is just the opposite of what most clients want us to do. If they have stores that are loosing money, they want us to devote our time to turning them around. The truth is that there are usually much greater problems in those loser stores than just marketing. And even if there are not, you'll find that it takes two to three times more effort to gain an increase in sales from loosing stores than from your top stores. Does that mean that you should ignore the loosers? Absolutely not. But there is a more profitable way to allocate your effort.

The end result of using a Streetfighting program for your stores is to increase profit. Do the owners or the shareholders care where the profit comes from as long as it comes? Probably not. So, why not concentrate your efforts in your better stores, where it take much less effort to add sales? Generating an extra 10 percent in successful stores puts a lot more on the bottom line of the company's books and does it faster than turning around losers. The top-down strategy allows you to show a return on your investment as soon as possible. Once you have those increased sales from your better stores, you can concentrate on the bottom 20 percent. With the top 20 percent showing real growth, and the bottom 20 percent starting to turn around, there is great pressure on the middle 60 percent to start paying attention. They're getting pressure from above and below them.

Another advantage of starting with your better stores is that it allows you to experience just how much improvement there can be. If your best stores start doing significantly better, your expectations of what all of your stores can do rise dramatically. Also, you'll get a lot more actual successes from the better stores faster, which helps in the roll-out process.

Maintain Your Program

As you roll out your program you'll need to put a maintenance plan in place. Once a manager is up and running, you want to have a Streetfighter trainer keep in touch with that manager from time to time to ensure that he or she continues to follow the program. During the initial training that manager is contacted by phone every week, and he or she meets with a group once a month. In a maintenance situation, you may have phone conversations with your managers once every two to three weeks and hold group sessions once a quarter. Eventually you may want to spread out your calls and group meetings even more, but to spread them out too thin invites trouble for your program.

The danger period occurs after the first year when the novelty of Streetfighting wears off and the initial gains have been made. Then managers might have a tendency to pull back on the program and look at other things. For this reason your maintenance program is critical. You've gone through development and rollout. Maintenance, by comparison, is relatively easy, and without it all that effort you put into instituting the program could be wasted.

We've discovered while training people that one trainer can effectively handle up to fifty managers at one time. In a maintenance situation that number can go up because the number of calls and meetings is reduced. Also, if the program has been planned properly, the area supervisors are doing their part to maintain the program.

Keeping fifty managers and their stores and their marketplaces all straight can be challenging. Many companies find it useful to use a computer and client-contact-management software.

A good software package allows you to keep track of each location, the phone numbers of the managers, the types of promotions that the location has done, your last date of contact, and your projected next date of contact. The software also should help you to keep notes about each location's Streetfighter campaign, and to send memos and letters to location managers, and to regional, divisional, and corporate bosses.

There are also some very low-tech tools you can use to help you better advise your managers. Every time you add a new manager and/or store to your program, ask him or her to send you a city map marked with the location of his or her store, other stores you own in the area, and the stores of competitors. Also request a copy of the local Yellow Pages. By looking at the advertisers in various categories, you can get a good idea of the potential cross-promotion partners for that store. For example, if you have found that full-service car washes are a strong cross-promotional partner for your business, you could look up car washes in the Yellow Pages. You could then get an idea of the number and location of full-service car washes in your new manager's area, a subject to pursue in a future conversation with that manager. The store manager might have a better knowledge of how useful a particular car wash would be, but your knowledge of this topic would certainly help to get the ball rolling. Moreover, you will gain credibility with that manager because you have impressed him or her with your knowledge of the local marketplace.

Call the local Chamber of Commerce to get its information package, including a list of major employers in the area and a list of nonprofit organizations. Ask your manager to give you a list of all the news media in the area; you'll need this to give him or her good advice about getting publicity. You might also consider getting a Sunday subscription to the local daily newspaper. Scanning the local Sunday paper gives you an idea of what's going on in the community, and what's going on can often prompt promotional ideas.

Obviously, if you're keeping tabs on fifty store managers, that's an awful lot of material to review, but such a review is very helpful when you're doing most of your consulting and training over the phone. And keep in mind that because you'll probably have a number of stores in the same marketplace, you won't have to do an in-depth review for every store. Once you have familiarized yourself with the market conditions for one of your locations in a particular city, you can use that information while keeping in touch with your other managers in that area.

This approach has one other advantage. Some promotions that you set up could benefit all the stores in a given marketplace. While the Streetfighter focus is on the individual store in its individual neighborhood, Streetfighter promotions can be linked together to form a chain of promotions. A case in point is the two-way promotion that was conducted by Minit-Lube and Skippers, a fast-food fish restaurant chain. The promotion was initiated by a Minit Lube manager for his store. One thing led to another, and eventually the promotion was picked up by all the Minit Lube and Skippers locations in the Portland and Seattle markets.

With all this structure, you still need to keep in mind that the most important aspect of teaching and advising the store managers is your own personal experience with the Streetfighter techniques. You need to become a Streetfighter yourself before you can expect to effectively teach or motivate anyone else to become a Streetfighter. Prior to beginning your program, choose a store and serve as its designated Streetfighter for a few months. Learn the neighborhood and set up the promotions yourself. That experience will be invaluable. Work on setting up a variety of promotions. Include cross-promotions, value cards, employee contests, a fundraiser, and an event promotion. Also work on getting some publicity for the store and perhaps instituting a customer-referral program.

Then you can use examples taken from your own experience in your program. Be careful not to sound like you are the be-all and end-all to this type of marketing. It's easy to turn off managers if you come on too strong or toot your own horn too much. You should give the store manager you originally worked with much of the credit for the success of promotions. When I present such information I use the term "You" instead of "I."

When everything is up and running you still have to keep an effort going or the program will eventually fade away. Refresher courses help. Hold regular Streetfighter panel discussions and presentations at your annual convention. Give out a Streetfighter of the Year award. Keep your Streetfighter newsletter going. Share successes with the rest of the store managers. Also, to make sure that your managers will stay adventurous and won't be afraid to try something bold and new, and also to demonstrate that not every attempt is going to work out, give out some "spoof" awards for the biggest mistakes of the year. Make this a fun event, but at the same time reinforce the idea that the only way to make advancements is by not being afraid to fail.

16

Case History: The Athlete's Foot

This chapter was a joy to write. It's an example of what can happen to a Streetfighter Marketing program when management supports it. The examples in this chapter are all actual accounts of promotions done by The Athlete's Foot franchisees.

The Athlete's Foot is an international franchise of athletic shoe retailers whose stores are located primarily in major malls. Their stores are independently owned by the franchisees and supported by the franchisor. Over the years, The Athlete's Foot has conducted a wide variety of promotional programs, adapted and geared specifically to their business and their marketplaces. This chapter shares a number of their ideas. You'll see that the root of their ideas are similar to the promotional ideas presented in this book. What's of great interest is the variety of their franchisees who made them work.

At The Athlete's Foot the Streetfighter marketing program is a major part of the total marketing effort, complimenting their more traditional forms of advertising. Every three months The Athlete's Foot puts out a Streetfighter packet containing the best of the promotions that were done for that quarter that could be used by other franchisees. Streetfighting promotions are also recognized in their publications and at their convention.

The following are ideas that they've shared with their franchisees and now they share with you:

Athlete of the Week. For eight weeks, The Athlete's Foot congratulated the local "Athlete of the Week" with a gift certificate for $50. In the newspaper each week an ad ran next to the announcement of that week's chosen athlete.

Nutrisystem Cross-Promotion. Nutrisystem members were rewarded with coupons for reaching their goals: 5 percent off an Athlete's Foot purchase for losing five pounds, 10 percent off for loosing ten pounds, and 15 percent off for loosing fifteen pounds in the sixty-day period the promotion ran. In addition, Nutrisystems' employees were provided with 20 percent coupons and T-shirts to encourage their promotion of the program. As a result of the strong relationship established with that Nutrisystem franchisee, the store was later invited to participate in a four-hour, live, remote radio broadcast from The Athlete's Foot store, during which the Nutrisystem store received numerous mentions.

Ticket to Event. The franchisee in Oshkosh, Wisconsin, took advantage of a sporting event with an international flavor. Tickets were purchased for the basketball game between the Soviet Union's Spartak team and the University of Wisconsin at Oshkosh's team and were given away to shoppers. The franchisee received free mentions in print and radio advertisements for the game.

Mall-Walking Clinics. The store hosted mall-walking clinics twice a week for one month. Mall walkers were given the opportunity to "test drive" shoes once a week. Information sheets on walking, dieting, and proper clothing were distributed. A T-shirt was given to each participant.

Community Involvement. The owner of four stores in Iowa and Illinois spent several years promoting his business to runners. Through continual efforts, including a special certificate for members of local running clubs, he has made a big impact on that segment of the athletic footwear market. A special price was offered to local running clubs on elective safety vests.

Walking Clinic II. A store hosted a walking clinic and invited two local podiatrists to speak. Drawings for two pairs of walking shoes were held during the clinic. The promotion was supported through television, radio, and newspaper ads. The store sold over three hundred pairs of walking shows that year, more than any other store in the chain. Moreover, the podiatrists started sending their patients to the stores.

Youth Education Rewards. A store rewarded students in two local elementary schools with tickets to a major league baseball game. Every student who received an "A" in any major subject received two free tickets (one for a parent). Corporate mentions at the games were negotiated and public relations was used to support the program.

Shoe Prescription Card. The Newark, Delaware, franchisee joined forces with a local podiatrist to create a small piece that would serve as a message to his patients. This 4 1/4" x 4 1/2" printed card was placed in the waiting room of the doctor's office and handed out in the office to patients with specific needs in athletic footwear. On recommendation from the doctor, patients were given this card, which lists specific problems, and invited to visit The Athlete's Foot store, which has a fit technician on staff. An added incentive in the form of a 10 percent savings was offered inside the fold out card.

Catalogue. The Athlete's Foot developed and distributed a catalogue to its family-plan members. Copies were also handed out in the stores. The catalogue included all types of information, including technical specifics, importance of proper fit, categorical advice, fitness tips, and so on. All product categories were highlighted.

Bounce-Back Program. For three weeks The Athletes's Foot distributed a "Special Savings Card" to customers during the spring new-product roll out, offering a 15 percent discount. A two-week redemption period during an off-sale time was used to help drive sales. The card was successful in gaining repeat visits from the customers.

Win Big with The Athlete's Foot. Taking advantage of its college-campus location, a franchisee with six stores throughout the Madison and Milwaukee, Wisconsin, developed a creative promotion tied into the local women's college basketball team. Every time the team won, the store would offer a discount equal to its winning-point margin. Thus a two-point win produced a 2 percent discount and a twenty-point win produced a 20 percent discount. The ad was placed in the gamebook for each of the ten home games. Unfortunately (or fortunately), the team has yet to win at home!

Baseball Fever. An Athletes' Foot franchisee sponsored a "Baseball Fever" promotion to support the local college baseball team. For every run the team scored during a given game in April, the store offered a dollar off the customer's next purchase. The promotion was supported through radio ads and in-store signs. Sales were up significantly during this promotion, including one day when sales reached $6,000.

Free Disneyland Trip Contest. The owner of stores in Marysville and Mount Vernon, Washington, used a promotion in which customers were invited to visit either of his two stores and register to win a free trip to Disneyland. He used newspaper ads with a bounce-back certificate good for $10 off any regularly priced shoes of $40 or more.

Soccer Ball Giveaway. An Athlete's Foot gave away a free soccer ball with the purchase of a specific soccer shoe. The offer was promoted on a flyer distributed in registration packets for thirty local soccer teams. The store sold out of the shoe. The promotion was so successful that suggestions were made to adapt it to other sports, including basketball, baseball, and tennis.

Ticket Giveaway. The store gave away tickets to a major league baseball game with every purchase of $50 or more. Tickets to a popular team's games have a high value to its fans. You can also adapt this strategy to attract different types of audiences by giving away tickets to concerts or other types of events.

Mailer to Family-Plan Members. Another store did a promotion utilizing its mailing list of family-plan members. It offered them a prepurchase discount program. A bounce-back certificate was offered in the mailing to provide additional incentive.

NCAA Basketball Tournament Contest. The franchisee, whose University Square store is located on the campus of the University of Wisconsin at Madison, set up an NCAA Tournament contest in partnership with the college newspaper. In print ads, students were invited to stop into the store and pick up an entry form. Each contestant was to fill out the bracket sheet to make his or her predictions up through the championship game. At the conclusion of the NCAA Tournament, contestants' total points for accuracy of their predictions were added up. The first-place winner won a $100 gift certificate, the second-place winner a $50 gift certificate, and the third-place winner a $25 gift certificate. More than one thousand people entered the competition, increasing store traffic dramatically.

Road Race Sponsorship. One owner with twenty-four stores throughout Arkansas, Oklahoma, and Texas sponsored the Pacificares Centennial Land Run. This race was the culmination of three full days of festivities celebrating the historic Oklahoma Land Rush of 1889. As part of the sponsorship package, the store owner received twenty 10-second TV spots and one 30-second spot during a prime-time special.

Sales Incentive of Overstocks, Discontinueds, and Slow Movers. This was a price-coded promotion designed by a franchisee in Guam to rid himself of otherwise useless inventory. All the unwanted shoes were price-coded to end in 88¢. Employees were paid $2.00 for each of the price-coded "and 88¢" shoes they sold. The employee was required to bring out two pairs of "and 88¢" shoes with each regular priced shoe, thus presenting a minimum of three pairs of shoes to each customer. As a result of this employee incentive the franchisee rid himself of five hundred pairs of unwanted shoes during the special sale.

Lucky Draw with Purchase. In a Hong Kong franchise, Christmas purchases of over $50 during the month of December were encouraged by a contest. A total of one hundred draw cards, ten of which were numbered, were placed inside a draw box. The lucky customers who picked one of the ten numbered cards were awarded gifts according to the number that was drawn. The gifts were donated by vendors. The promotion was supported with in-store signs consisting of a foamboard listing all the prizes and details and placed in the front window. Direct-mail pieces were delivered to increase customer awareness.

Gift Set with Purchase. Two stores in Singapore and one in Malaysia wanted to entice higher volumes of sales during the holiday period. The owners awarded customers who purchased more than $150 of merchandise gift sets consisting of a variety of items such as caps, T-shirts, and shoe bags imprinted with The Athlete's Foot logo.

T-Shirt Giveaway. In Springfield, Illinois, a local fitness center, as part of its grand-opening festivities, gave away Athlete's Foot T-shirts. The store logo was on the back and the fitness center logo on the front. A total of 167 shirts were given away at a cost to the franchisee of just under $3 each.

Customer Appreciation. A franchisee with stores in Greenville, Jackson, Tupelo, and Vicksburg, Mississippi, had put sixty-two special certificates with $50, $20, $10, and $5 values in a draw box in each of his stores. When a customer bought any footwear selling at regular price, he or she draw from the box. The savings indicated on the card was applied to that purchase. Employees with a $50 winner received $15 and those with $20 winners got $5. This promotion was advertised with print and radio ads, and also with in-store signs. The promotion got the employees to work extra hard selling shoes in hopes that their customer would get a $50 or a $20 certificate.

Basketball Shoot-Out. A Quincy, Illinois, franchisee created an annual event at his mall, and used TV and newspaper advertising to promote it. During this three-day promotion potential customers were invited to shoot five free-throws to win discounts and a free Nike basketball. If the customer made one shot he or she got a 5 percent discount; two out of five baskets won a 10 percent discount; and so on.

Year's Supply of Free Shoes. The store owner in Rhinelander, Wisconsin, came up with an alternative to the coupon wars by having a contest within the friendly confines of the store. He held a pre-Christmas drawing with the lucky winner getting one pair of shoes a month for a year.

YMCA Promotion. The owner in Aberdeen, South Dakota, teamed up with his local YMCA to offer a 25 percent savings to prospective customers when they purchased a one-year membership at the YMCA. Radio spots ran during the month of November.

Quiz Bowl Game. The manager in St. Thomas, the Virgin Islands, invited students from the Virgin Island's high schools to call in and play the Quiz Bowl Game. A range of questions had to be answered correctly. Those students with all the correct answers received a gift certificate from the store. This event was promoted with internal posters at all Virgin Island high schools, and with radio, print, and TV spots.

Conclusion. This was just a sampling of some of the Streetfighter Marketing tactics used by The Athlete's Foot franchisees around the world. They've adapted the techniques to fit their product and their marketplace. A book, tape series, or seminar can only be the starting point for this type of program. You then have to take it to the next level by adaptation and implementation. The franchisor should be complimented for supporting his or her neighborhood marketing program with his or her effort and investment. The franchisees should be complimented for taking advantage of the opportunities to increase their sales on a shoestring budget.

Notes

1.   Area of Dominate Influence, a term used by Arbitron to designate a television viewing area. An ADI often includes the metro area along with all the area suburbs and small towns where that television viewing signal is dominant.

2.   Giant Advertising, 1041 W. 18th Street, Costa Mesa, CA, 800/648-7907; 714/640-2259; fax 714/650-2116.

3.   *How to Remember Names* by Thomas Crook, Harber Prenial; *On Your Way To Remembering Names & Faces* (audio) by Bob Burg, 800/726-3667.

4.   *Successful Retail Selling* and *Managing a Retail Staff to Success* (audio or video) by Harry Friedman, self published, The Friedman Group, 8636 Sepulveda Boulevard, Suite C, Los Angeles, CA 90045. 800/351-8040.

5.   C.P.C. Associates, 33 Rock Hill Road, Bala Cynwyd, PA 19004; 215/667-1780; fax 25/667-5650

6.   Fortunately Yours, 800-337-1889; 614/337-1889; fax 614/231-8889 326 Vista Dr. Gahanna, OH 43230

7.   Standard Rates & Data Service.

8.   "Signs for the Times," *Remodeling*, February 1994, p. 98.

Resource Guide

The Advertising Kit: A Complete Guide for Small Business, by Jeannette Smith. New York: Lexington Books, 1994. 800/323-2336.

Blitz Call, The, by Bill Truax and Sue Truax. Book, audiotape, and workbook set. Chagrin Falls, Ohio: Trufield Publishing; 216/248-6242; Fax: 216/498-0052.

Comlink. A device that allows your computer modem (using TeleMagic) to dial directly through most phone systems. 800/869-1420.

Customerization, by Murray Raphel. Self-published book. Gordon's Alley, Atlantic City, N.J.: Murray Raphel Advertising, 1993. 609/348-6646.

Fast Forward: How to Do a Lot More Business in a Lot Less Time, by Dr. Michael LeBoeuf. Book and audiotape. New York: Putnam & Sons, 1994.

Giant Advertising Inflatable balloons and blimps. 1041 W. 18th Street, Costa Mesa, CA; 800/648-7907; 714/640-2259; Fax 714/650-2116.

GMP: The Greatest Management Principle in the World, by Dr. Michael LeBoeuf. Paperback. New York: Berkley Publishing Group, Audio album available from Nightingale-Conant, 7300 N. Leheigh Ave., Chicago; 800/323-5552; in Illinois, call 312/647-0300. Video available from Coronet/MTI Film & Video, Deerfield, IL; 800/621-2131.

Great Brain Robbery, by Murray Raphel and Ray Considine. Self-published book. Gordon's Alley, Atlantic City, NJ: Murray Raphel Advertising, 609/348-6646.

Guerrilla Marketing: Secrets for Making Big Profits from Your Small Business, by Jay Conrad Levinson. Book. Boston: Houghton Mifflin, 1984.

Guerrilla Marketing Attack: New Strategies, Tactics, and Weapons for Winning Big Profits from Your Small Business, by Jay Conrad Levinson. Book. Boston: Houghton Mifflin, 1989.

Guerrilla Selling, by Bill Galligar, Orval Ray Wilson and Jay Conrad Levinson. Book. Boston: Houghton Mifflin, 1993.

How to Get the Most Out of Trade Shows, by Steve Miller. Available directly from the author: 33422 30th Avenue SW, Federal Way, WA 98027; 206/874-9665; Fax 206/874-9666

How to Win Customers and Keep Them for Life, by Dr. Michael LeBouef, Book and audiotape. Video available through Cally Curtis Company, Hollywood, CA, Can be ordered through the author, 504/833-8873.

How to Work a Room: A Guide to Successfully Managing the Mingling, by Susan RoAne. Book. Audio available through the RoAne Group, 14 Wilder Street, Suite 100, San Francisco, CA 94131; 415/239-2224.

Intel SatisFAXion Modem/400 Allows you to send and receive faxes directly on your computer. Intel Corporation, 5200 N.E. Elam Young Parkway, Hilsboro, OR; 97124-6497, 503/696-8080; 800/538-3373; 800/458-6231; Fax: 503/629-7580.

Managing a Retail Staff to Success, by Harry Friedman. Self-published book. The Friedman Group, 8636 Sepulveda Boulevard, Suite C, Los Angeles, CA 90045; 800/351-8040.

Managing the Future: Ten Driving Forces of Change for the '90s, by Robert B. Tucker. Book. New York: G. P. Putnam & Sons, 1991.

Million Dollar Presentations, by Bill Bishop. Audiotape; replaces the *Million Dollar Close* program. Available directly from the author: Bill Bishop & Associates, 834 Gran Paseo Drive, Orlando, FL 32825; 407/281-1395.

Mind Your Own Business, by Murray Raphel Self-published book. Gordon's Alley, Atlantic City, NJ: Murray Raphel Advertising, 609/348-6646.

Novell NetWare Version 3.12, by Network Computing Products. Local Area Network (LAN) allows all of your computers to share information and printers as well as numerous other functions. Very important when using TeleMagic and WordPerfect on more than one computer. 122 East 1700 South, Provo, UT 84606; 801/429-7000; 800/453-1267.

Perfect Sales Presentation, by Robert L. Shook. Book. New York: Bantam Books, 1987.

Phone Power, by George Walther. Book can be ordered directly from the author. 6947 Coal Creek Parkway, S.E. #100, Renton, WA 98059; 206/255-2900; Fax 206/235-6360. Also available on audio cassettes.

Plantronics. Telephone headsets that enable hands-free operations. 345 Encinal Street, Santa Cruz, CA 95060; 800/544-4660, 408/426-5868.

Power Speak, by Dorothy Leeds. Book. New York: Prentice-Hall, Book, audio album (self-published), and video can be ordered from the author: Organization Technologies, Inc., 800 West End Avenue, Suite 10A, New York, NY 10025; 212/864-2424.

Prime Prospects Unlimited, by Bill Bishop (Formally called *Gold Calling.*). Self-published set of eight audio cassettes. Bill Bishop & Associates, 834 Gran Paseo Drive, Orlando, FL 32825; 407/281-1395.

Profitable Telemarketing: Total Training for Professional Excellence, by George Walther. Six cassette tapes. Can be ordered directly from the author: 6947 Coal Creek Parkway, S.E. #100, Renton , WA 98059; 206/255-2900; Fax 206/235-6360.

Public Relations Writer's Handbook, by Merry Aronson and Don Spetner. New York: Lexington Books, 1994; 800-232-2336.

Secrets of Savvy Networking, by Susan RoAne. The RoAne Group, 14 Wilder Street, Suite 100, San Francisco, CA 94131; 415/239-2224.

Smart Questions, by Dorothy Leeds. Book. New York: McGraw-Hill, Book, audiotape (self-published), and video can be ordered from the author: Organizational Technologies, Inc., 800 West End Avenue, Suite 10A, NY, NY 10025; 212/864-2424.

Stalls are for Horses, not Sales People, by Bill Bishop. Self published set of two audio cassettes. 834 Gran Paseo Drive, Orlando, FL 32825; 407/281-1395.

Streetfighter's Profit Package, The. An audio/video/book training system with telephone consulting and support from the authors.

VIDEO: *Streetfighter's Neighborhood Sales Builders*: One-hour VHS.

AUDIO: *Streetfighter's Neighborhood Sales Builders*: Six audio cassettes with workbook.

AUDIO: *Streetfighter's How to Get Clients*: Six audio cassettes.

AUDIO: *The 33 Secrets of Street Smart Tele-Selling*: Three audio cassettes and workbook.

BOOK: *Streetfighting: Low Cost Advertising/Promotion for Your Business*.

BOOK: *Street Smart Marketing*

PHONE SUPPORT: The Streetfighter's Profit Package includes one year of telephone consulting and support with Jeff & Marc Slutsky for questions, ideas, and review of promotions.

US $399.00. Available directly from the authors. 800-SLUTSKY. (800-758-8759) 614-337-7474. Fax 614-337-2233. Streetfighter Marketing, 467 Waterbury Court, Gahanna, OH 43230. Add $8.50 for UPS shipping and handling within the United States. Please increase the shipping amount accordingly when ordering from another country. Thirty-day money-back guarantee.

Successful Telephone Selling in the 90's, by Martin D. Shafiroff and Robert L. Shook. New York: Harper & Row, 1993.

Successful Retail Selling, by Harry Friedman. Self-published audiotape and video. Available from the author: The Friedman Group, 8636 Sepulveda Boulevard, Suite C, Los Angeles, CA 90045; 800/351-8040.

TeleMagic Telemarketing Computer Software. Telemarketing contact computer software for single user or network telemarketing program. Contact TeleMagic, Inc., 5928 Pascal Court, Suite 150, Carlsbad CA 92008; 800/835-MAGIC, 619/431-4000.

Upside Down Marketing, by George Walther. Book. New York: McGraw-Hill, 1994. Also available as a six-cassette audio album. Can be ordered directly from the author: 6947 Coal Creek Parkway, S.E. #100, Renton, WA 98059; 206/255-2900; Fax 206/235-6360.

Unabashed Self-Promoters Guide, by Dr. Jeffrey L. Lant. (39.50) Self-published. paperback. Revised edition, 1993. From Jeffrey Lant & Assoc., 617-547-6372, P.O. Box 38-2767, Cambridge, MA 02238.

Word-Of-Mouth Marketing, by Jerry R. Wilson. Book. New York: John Wiley & Sons, 1991. Available also through the author: 800/428-5666 or 317/257-6876.

Working Smart, by Dr. Michael LeBoeuf. New York: Warner Books, 1979. Time management and goal-setting techniques. *Working Smarter* available in audio from Nightingale-Conant.

WordPerfect Version 6.0. WordPerfect Corporation, 1555 North Technology Way, Orem UT, 84057-2399; 801/225-5000; Telex: 820618; Fax: 801/222-5077.

WordPerfect Presentations Version 2.0. WordPerfect Corporation, 1555 North Technology Way, Orem UT, 84057-2399; 801/225-5000; Telex: 820618; Fax: 801/222-5077.

WP-Merge Version 2.90 Allows you to use WordPerfect while in TeleMagic. Resource Dynamics, Inc., PO Box 66419, St. Petersburg, FL 33736; 813/367-1020, Fax: 813/367-8452.

Index